OUR HISTORY,
THEIR HISTORY,
WHOSE HISTORY?

SEAGULL
BOOKS
·
CELEBRATING
40 YEARS

THE INDIA LIST

ALSO AVAILABLE

ROMILA THAPAR
Voices of Dissent: An Essay

ROMILA THAPAR

OUR HISTORY,
THEIR HISTORY,
WHOSE HISTORY?

LONDON NEW YORK CALCUTTA

Seagull Books, 2023

First published by Seagull Books, 2023

© Romila Thapar, 2023

ISBN 978 1 8030 9 354 3

British Library Cataloguing-in-Publication Data
A catalogue record for this book is available from the British Library

Typeset by Seagull Books, Calcutta, India
Printed and bound by WordsWorth India, New Delhi, India

CONTENTS

PREFACE

This is an expanded version of the Dr C. D. Deshmukh Memorial Lecture that I gave at the India International Centre, New Delhi, on 14 January 2023. The lecture will be published in the *IIC Quarterly*.

I would like to thank the director of the IIC for giving me permission to publish this much-expanded version independently. Thanks also to the *Wire* for permission to republish the article entitled 'The "Rationalizing" of Indian History by the NCERT' as the Afterword in this book.

I would like to thank a few of my friends for taking the trouble to read the text of the initial lecture and commenting on it. My even greater thanks to Muzaffar Alam and Shirish Patel for commenting on this much-expanded version, involving more time and concentration.

Needless to say that I much appreciate Naveen Kishore and the editors of Seagull Books suggesting that they publish the expanded version of the lecture.

Romila Thapar
May Day, 2023

For history is the raw material for nationalist or ethnic or fundamentalist ideologies, as poppies are the raw material for heroin addiction. The past is an essential element, perhaps the essential element, in these ideologies. If there is no suitable past, it can always be invented.

Eric Hobsbawm
On History (1998)

OUR HISTORY,
THEIR HISTORY,
WHOSE HISTORY?

1

Nationalism encourages a variety of narratives about the past of the society from which it emerges. These narratives differ as their intention is not so much to focus on any particular history, but to provide ancestry to the communities involved in the nationalist enterprise of the society, and to give the society a focal point to where it should head. Differing identities projected by diverse nationalisms result in projections that are not identical. Some of the generalizations thus projected and claiming to be based on history have to be tested for reliability by historians. If there is little or no evidence to support them, then this gives rise to controversies between professional historians and others who claim to know history. Generalizations intended to excite the wider society, and flavoured sometimes with absurdities, are naturally ignored by professional historians. Not every narrative about the past is valid history. Readings of the past have to be based on proven, reliable evidence and the causal connections they make have to be logical and to draw on rational argument. Misrepresenting the views of professional historians is another way of drawing the attention of the media to oneself. This is commonly resorted to by non-historians, especially those seeking publicity. Such misrepresentations are generally ignored by professional historians as ignorant flippancy, and in any case demanding reliable evidence from most non-historians would be rather like discussing the subject with a wall.

Perhaps I should preface my discussion by explaining what I am referring to in the title of this text rather than leaving it a trifle enigmatic. History is no longer what it once was, namely, collecting information from a body of texts and composing it into a chronological narrative. Critical inquiry based on an analysis of the sources is now essential to the writing of history. How this is to be done constitutes part of the methodology of history that all professional historians should be familiar with. History in India written by trained professional historians is that based on an accepted methodology, which in its analyses follows the procedures of research in the social sciences.

Opposed to professional historians are those untrained in historical methodology who fantasize about the past. They present what they would like to believe to be the picture of the past. This takes us back to the eighteenth and nineteenth centuries, when history was the narrative of events and persons associated with an event, all shuffled into chronological order. It is more often that which gives support to a particular ideology, frequently political, and is suited to the narrow nationalism that it is meant to endorse. Whether it has any evidence to support the particular past that it constructs is irrelevant to its purpose. Its concern is not with comprehending the past as a form of knowledge about the world we live in. Its concern is with using the past effectively for political purposes, and even inventing it, should this be necessary to its purpose. This past must be so constructed as to sustain the political ideology for which it is foundational. Inevitably, these two approaches are in conflict: as between the professional historian who demands proven evidence for any construction of the past and the person who insists that the past as constructed by him or her, however casually, is authentic.

It hardly needs reiterating that there's currently a fierce battle raging between professional historians and those who are untrained in the methodology of researching history yet claim to have expertise in history. There are a handful of those that are not professional historians but who do have a knowledge of the methodology of writing history. Such exceptions are rare and they are persons with whom historians can have a dialogue. Among them, D. D. Kosambi was a mathematician by profession but was a leading scholar in using the required methodology when writing on ancient history, and was a remarkably fine historian. The fundamental differentiation is between those that insist on checking the reliability of the evidence quoted and others who pay little or no attention to providing such evidence.

Disregarding the evidence disables one from asking the questions that history as a social science requires for research and historical interpretation. It also disables one from recognizing that the structure of society, and the interplay of events that the professional historian constructs, is complex and born out of interdisciplinary research. It cannot be dismissed, as is commonly done in popular history today in India, by insisting that such research is merely a Marxist explanation of the past. A Marxist analysis is not just any attempt at giving attention to the study of society and economy; it uses a particular pattern of analysis in examining social and economic connections that shape society. Therefore, every discussion of social and economic factors in the construction of history is not automatically Marxist, since every socio-economic study does not necessarily conform to the same pattern. The approach of Max Weber, for instance, also focuses on explaining how a society and economy function, and it is quite distinct from Marxist theory. The same can be said for other theories. The use of methods from the social sciences enables one to expand the range of questions and to search for more extensive sources that might provide more meaningful answers. It broadens the study to assess the priorities in more than one explanation. Hence the importance of interdisciplinary research. The purpose of history is not limited to telling a story. It has to explain the past and attempt to answer as many questions about the past as are asked.

Since I have referred to historical methodology, I should briefly explain what I mean by this term. It means asking how one proceeds to investigate a subject and to search in one's explanations for the logical and rational. Having found a theme and a central question to investigate, one proposes a hypothesis. I would remind myself that I should proceed with what I have called the four *a*'s: artefact, author, agenda and audience. That is not the full gamut but it makes a starter. The expanse of possible enquiries would attempt to explore questions relating to *what? when? where?* and *why?* The expanse of the inquiry becomes obvious.

Artefact was the source that could be a text in any form or an object from various origins, and each had to be meticulously tested for veracity if used as evidence. Author referred to the person who created it—whether it be a bard or a potter—its materiality, its tradition and what it conveys. Agenda covered the agencies responsible for defining its purpose, as well as the intentions of the other three. Audience included both ends of the spectrum, involving the user as also the patron, whether the latter was the same or another. Putting this data into an order and categorizing the questions often took one to the point almost of asking the kinds of questions that brought more information.

The second stage was that of explaining and answering the question one had started with—the hypothesis. The explanation drew on logic and reasoning. At this point it was exciting to discover that what was loosely called the dialectical method, proposed by Socrates and followed even in modern philosophy, was actually fundamental to many Indian philosophical schools as well.

The debate began with setting out in detail the arguments of the *pratipaksha* / the opposite view, which was then juxtaposed with one's own or earlier arguments / *purvapaksha*, and through the debate between the two one might arrive at the *siddhanta* / solution. Knowledge can only advance if it is questioned. By the time one had done this exercise, there was enough to get started. More importantly, it provided a range of perspectives, some known and some unknown. And it was only the start!

2

The much-respected historian of modern Europe, Eric Hobsbawm, has commented on the relationship of history to nationalism. I have quoted the comment above. He argues that the past is an important input into those ideologies associated with the forms that nationalism takes, given that claims to histories become prolific in a society nurturing nationalisms. Fundamentalist ideologies use their own version of history as a source of legitimizing their explanations of the past. Should the required history be absent, it can always be invented. At one level, the past carries a necessary contribution to the creation of a nation and to justifying what is created as a nation. Hobsbawm expresses the relationship very succinctly when he writes that history is to nationalism what poppies are to a heroin addict. I would merely add that the dependence has to be recognized and analysed.

Origins have significance when the contemporary status of situations is being established. They generally acquire a higher status if they can be placed in the more remote past, as then they can be treated as 'tradition'. They still have to be legitimized by assessing evidence and accuracy. What comes from the poppy and enters the mind of the heroin addict conjures up fantasies about a generally magnificent past, or else a particular kind of past whose contours are determined by the specific requirements of the present, and, more pointedly, by a political ideology. This latter can have problems that need solutions, and in some situations the solutions are supposedly best found as coming from the past. The process is malleable and open to formulation as wished, and this fantasy sustains the present. Those who are familiar with the counter-currents of actual history as opposed to imagined history in the India of today, or indeed have smoked pot, might appreciate the parallel!

3

My purpose is to examine the link between history and particular kinds of nationalism. It could explain why there is a conflict between professional historians and those whose views of the past are unacceptable to the former. History is not static. A single explanation cannot be applied to all events through many centuries. History marks changes in a society. Both personalities and activities are diverse at various points in time, so this kaleidoscope requires constant adjustments to changing contexts. Some changes are slow and go through a lengthy evolution; others are faster and tend to punctuate the historical flow.

When nationalism was first beginning to be formulated as a concept a few centuries back, it was seen as encapsulating social and economic changes and others that were virtually inconceivable in earlier societies. I hope to show that nationalism can be a process, bringing together and uniting all the communities that inhabit a particular territory in support of a change in society or opposing a target common to all. This earlier form is what I would like to call a unitary, integrative nationalism that cut across communities and drew them together in a particular country to support a single purpose. An example of this would be the national movements in colonies that struggled to overthrow the colonial power and become independent nation-states.

This nationalism I would differentiate from the later forms in some countries which identified with units of society or communities according to certain common features, such as a particular religion or language, or caste or ethnicity. This nationalism, in contrast to the earlier one, chooses one qualifier from among a few identities—religion, language, ethnicity or whatever— as the identity through which it segregates the one from the other. I would therefore call it segregated nationalism, where each community is segregated and treated as having a distinctly different identity and its own separate goal. In this, the dominant nationalism is that of the community that has the largest numbers following a single identity.

There is therefore a clear difference between integrated nationalism, which attempts to bring together all the communities within a society into one new national identity, often named after the country or territory that it represents, and the other, which insists on the segregation of all the communities, naming them by traditional names for religions, languages, castes, or whatever keeps them distinct. In the second form of nationalism, the largest community in terms of numbers dominates society and its majoritarian agenda prevails. Diverse movements that draw on a single community among the many, and qualify nationalism by linking it to the identity of religion, language or ethnicity while excluding others, claim to be nationalisms of varying kinds. They also claim territories as nation-states in the same way as inclusive, integrated nationalism.

The question has been asked whether such identities can qualify as the basis of nationalisms or if the definition of nationalism is limited to one unified group. The question relates to a seeming pattern of history and chronology. Colonies that sustain a uniform, integrated nationalism and liberate themselves may have to face the segregated nationalism of the majority community making demands on the nation-state. Can one form of nationalism mutate into another? Indian nationalism was inclusive and integrated. But its opposite, Hindu nationalism is defined as exclusive and segregated. But this is not a mutation. Is it, then, the surfacing of another kind of nationalism? This question faces many states today and the form of the post-nationalism state is a matter of debate.

The origin of nationalism is among the foundational moments in modern history. It is a time when existing communities, generally constituting a kingdom or a colony, gradually shed their previous characteristics and morph, as it were, into a society that takes the form of a nation-state. Ideally, social and political hierarchies are discarded in favour of a relationship between citizen and state based on the rights and mutual obligations of both as recorded in the Constitution. Governance and its institutions have to be based on secular and democratic principles. This disqualifies religious nationalism as a situation that creates many problems. Communities come together in fresh ways. The coming together of communities in integrated nationalism posits a common past and anticipates a common future. For nationalism, the common future lies in the nation-state: a defined territory that incorporates all who live there ideally as equal and free members—but possibly not always so free and equal—of a new unit, namely, the nation.

History is brought in when the community that gives an identity to its nationalism insists on tracing its origins to a historical past, as most do. Cultures within this community are presumed to have common forms. Those sought to be excluded can be kept out by denying them these historical origins. The idea of nationalism can encapsulate the expressions of citizens who have a contracted relationship with the nation-state, such as through the Constitution. This is the record of the rights and obligations of both the citizens and the state to each other.

The establishment of this contract and the assumptions and procedures that go with it are entirely different from what had existed before. The fact of citizenship and its accompanying rights and duties were unthought of in earlier times. Nationalism, together with its accoutrements, is a foundational experience of modern times. This point should not be overlooked. In previous times, there were kingdoms ruled by kings and the people of the kingdom were the subjects of the king. With the coming of nationalism and the changes it brought, the people were no longer subjects of the king but were citizens of the nation-state: it implies a complete change of relationship to the state and to those governing the state. This is a profound change, the implication of which is not always understood; all too often the rights and obligations are not apprehended by the citizen, and the government reverts to what it was in monarchical times.

Cultures with a long history such as ours have been punctuated by points of historical change of varying intensity. These changes are not arbitrary. They have evolved and transformed our society as recorded by history. Nationalism itself is one of these seminal points of change. By definition, unitary nationalism should carry the entire population of a country in a nationalist movement that makes for a new and changed society, together with its multiple requirements and in keeping with the new contract on governance as set out in the founding Constitution. Nationalism is a concept that, when it comes to be adopted, terminates the old social system and brings in an alternative society with values, structures and divisions of powers that virtually revolutionize the existing society. Nationalism is meant to assist in the evoking and constructing of a new society and not merely be a resurrection of the old one. The new society is intended to be that of free citizens in an independent nation-state. Nationalist principles are actually not embedded in the ancient past, because the new society they give rise to is a response to current requirements, not to those that have long since passed away. They do not need legitimizing from the past. But any attempt to change the power structure in a society needs to underline its legitimacy—and one way of doing so is by drawing on the past which it claims as a part of this legitimacy.

Essential to integrated nationalism are other constituents: pre-eminently, democracy and secularism. These receive less attention in most nationalisms where constructing a new society requires refurbishing or replacing the old—to a lesser or greater degree. Democracy and secularism are taken as the basic difference between the old and the new. The functioning of a nation-state is seriously and negatively impacted where democracy and secularism are absent or given marginal importance, and where there is a tendency to endorse a mangled nationalism. Democracy treats the distribution of power among all citizens, given that all citizens have a say in this distribution through a representative government. Representation is of the opinion of citizens and is channelized through elections. Free and fair elections are essential to democracy, but defections of elected representatives from one party to another are not, and these latter disqualify the claims to democratic action. In governance, the rights and obligations of the Constitution have to be respected and practised. The freedom of speech and expression through public channels such as the media and in all institutions cannot be annulled.

Secularism ensures that religious concerns do not control civic activities and institutions.

The pattern that I have suggested of integrated and segregated nationalisms would seem to apply to India of the twentieth century. There was the all-inclusive national movement whose participants were from every community; its objectives were to maintain the unity of the Indian people and to overthrow colonial rule in order to become an independent, free nation-state. The other nationalism, segregated nationalism, was seeded in the 1920s and assumed the existence of two nations—the Hindu and the Muslim—which, it was argued, go back to the earliest times. Pakistan was built on the base of Muslim religious nationalism. The integrated nationalism succeeded in 1947 in bringing about independence, but its foundations needed strengthening, for we are now witnessing the strong presence of religious nationalism in the attempt to inaugurate a Hindu Rashtra in India. Bangladesh was carved out much later on the basis of another segregated nationalism—that of language.

4

Nationalism assumes that it brings about the uniting of communities on a substantial scale and, for the first time, in a new mode. The loyalty of citizens is to a new structure, namely, the nation-state. The single unitary purpose is the construction of the nation, that is of citizens forging a single national identity, for instance, when the Indian anti-colonial national movement struggled to establish a state consisting of free citizens equal in status and liberated from colonial control. It is difficult to envisage a condition of free and equal citizenship after millennia of subjecthood. Attempts were made to assist the change, as in the writing of the Constitution, adult franchise and the crucial direction given to the economy, but it seems now that they were not done with sufficient insistence.

The recognized concept was that of the unitary, integrated nationalism that was a single identity linking the territory together with its people, as does the state with its citizens. The single identity indicates a unitary nationalism focusing on all the citizens as a unity. In the Indian case, the initial uniting nationalism was anti-colonialism. But concepts can and often do sprout variant forms. In this case, and by contrast, there emerged a different category that admits divergent identities in the same society as units of a nationalist polity.

This other kind of nationalism confronts multiple identities, sometimes even in competition; and this context of multiform, segregated nationalism is more complicated. The community with the largest numbers adhering to the single chosen identity is given the highest ranking. It therefore demarcates not only the identity of a particular majority nationalism but also claims for it the highest status and privileges of citizenship. The majoritarianism required for multiform segregated nationalism is inherently opposed to democracy and secularism. The two kinds of nationalism have to be viewed as distinctly different and with distinctly different agendas, often contradictory.

In India, the divergence between the two has its own history. There was the single, unitary anti-colonial nationalism generally dated to the late nineteenth century, which had its own path and continued to be viewed as the sole form of nationalism. It supported a secular democratic programme for independent India. This perspective continued into the period of Independence and the establishment of the nation-state. Meanwhile, from the 1920s onwards, there arose a different nationalism for which the identity was religion. Its appeal was to members of the majority community—Hindus; alternately, the other exclusive nationalism was addressed to members of the largest of the minority communities—Muslims.

The organizations that supported this kind of nationalism qualified by religious identity were less anti-colonial, if at all, and instead increasingly antagonistic towards each other. The Hindus were larger in number and the Muslims were the largest of the minority religious groups. These two religion-based nationalisms were founded on the colonial construction of India which was said to consist of two nations—the Hindu and the Muslim. The trajectory of unitary nationalism was just the one nation-state. Multiple religious nationalisms were tied to creating more than one nation-state. In India it was initially two—India and Pakistan—and ultimately a third—Bangladesh.

The agenda of the integrated anti-colonial nationalism was the ideological movement for Independence. What kind of society was it intending to build? At Independence, when the polity mutated from kingdoms and the colony of earlier times into a single independent nation-state, unitary nationalism required the necessary presence of democracy and secularism qualifying the nation-state. As a citizen, every person was to have equal status and equal rights. There was to be no discrimination on any grounds. Inevitably, democracy and secularism were recognized as implicit in the functioning of the nation-state and became essential to the rights of the citizen. These rights had never existed before. Societies of the past did not give every person the right to be legally equal or to have a free status. The caste rules of the *Dharma-shastra*s, for instance, underlined and imprinted inequality, and thus the absence of such freedom. Islam too spoke of the equality of all in the eyes of Allah but the laws of Sharia introduced inequality among people living in the same society.

Where a nation-state comes into existence, the people cease to be subjects of a ruler or a kingdom and become citizens of the state. The two are quite different. This is a foundational change but not always recognized or fully observed. Democracy is adopted as the model polity. This implies that governing the state is dependent on the wishes of the people who are represented in various state bodies. Power lies not only with those that govern but is distributed among different agencies that represent the citizens—the judiciary, the legislature, the executive. The rules of government cannot be the arbitrary wishes of the rulers, since governance requires constitutional authority. Citizens elect their representatives who ideally debate the issues and take decisions reflective of the wishes of those who elected them. The rules and intentions of the functioning of the state are fenced within the Constitution which thereby should become the source of power and authority.

These are changes that call for foundational adjustments. Where such adjustments are not made, there we can say that either the required change is genuinely not understood or that there is a conscious effort to subvert it. Citizens at every level have to be aware of such adjustments being made, and if they are lacking, then the lack has to be explained. Hence the emphasis on citizens' rights and freedoms and the need for public discussions of these.

If we as Indians had understood this in 1947, we would have given more attention to these essentials and perhaps less to the redefining of religious identities. Instead, we went back to the narrow confines of battling over the pre-eminence of religious identities—a battle that continues even in the changed context of the present. The major thrust of 1947 was seen more as smoothening religious confrontations rather than with laying the foundations of the nation-state. A few politicians in positions of power did see the difference and gave priority to nation building, but most gradually went back to giving prominence to the centrality in our public life of religious issues and, on occasion, to encouraging conflict between religious communities. Politics based on community identities saw the new nation-state as the platform from which to assert these identities—religious, linguistic, caste, ethnic—that became the basis of segregation and majoritarianism. Gradually, religion and religious differences were made pre-eminent.

Necessary to nation-building was the planting and nourishing of the rights of citizens. The constitution also records these fundamental rights—the rights and obligations essential to all nation-states and their citizens, but which we observe only to varying degrees or not at all. These are rights to essentials: food, water and shelter; well-being such as healthcare and education; and to essentials of an equally important kind—such as the freedom of speech and expression, equality before the law and social justice in the practice of the rights applicable to all.

Nationalism, when it is integrated and unitary, should unite the people of a country. When the nation-state had been established in India, anti-colonial Indian nationalism had to consider the ways in which the functioning of the state would strengthen secular democracy. Other categories of specifically qualified and segregated nationalisms are obviously not intended to unify citizens but to allow them differentiated rights according to the relevant identity. Segregation often means that primary status is given to the group that adds up to being the majority. The agendas of these two types of nationalisms are distinct and need to be recognized as such. The specific identity among the many of a qualified nationalism is distinct from the single, unitary, inclusive nationalism that represents the aspirations of all citizens. The specific identity becomes the key factor in segregated nationalism. The turn to history is in order to claim the legitimacy and status of the current identities by dating them back to ancient times. The older they are said to be, the greater the status that they are supposed to have.

It is therefore with the emergence of diverse segregated nationalisms, with their versions of history required to justify their own political ambitions, and the politics of identity, that there develops a difference, in some cases even a confrontation, in how the past is viewed and presented. Thus, professional historians, basing themselves on methodological training and procedures in researching history, hold different views from those who are not trained historians yet preach a non-researched narrative of the past that they have casually put together as a form of nationalism. The intentions are obviously dissimilar. Central to accepting the statement presented by anyone as an explanation of the past is the need to recognize the purpose behind the explanation. It could have more to do with trying to legitimize a present situation than with a neutral representation of what happened. The multiform group is more dependent on public support, hence its concern with addressing and convincing social media as its primary and most attractive audience. It tries to reformulate history to uphold the assertions of the specific articulate majority among the citizens who are given priority in their nationalism. Other members of society who are not of the majority identity matter less unless they are the specific community being targeted as the enemy within society. With the coming of Independence, the colonial power is no longer the enemy. If the purpose is to uphold a specific majoritarian identity, then another enemy has to be found. It is usually the foremost among the minorities that are projected as the enemy of the majority community. History becomes crucial in such situations to argue for the primacy of the majority community identified by religion and its role in leading the campaign for the nation-state that will emerge from religious nationalism. The past has to be made subservient to the politics of contemporary times. This becomes the prerogative of those who are not trained in the methodology of researching history, as is easily recognizable by what they put forward as their version of history, which is largely wishful thinking unsupported by evidence.

In previous times, the study and writing of history in various forms were left to scholars from whose midst arose professional historians. History was then a narrative of past events and personalities. This pattern went back to the first millennium AD, to the *charitas* / historical biographies and *vamshavalis* / chronicles written in Sanskrit, and continued into the second millennium AD. Similar categories of narratives from Persian texts came next. Colonial history up to a point continued this trend but also added statements, explaining, in accordance with its perspective, the nature of the colony they were governing and how best to do it. This was the entry point of some of their more influential theories. Indian historians of the late nineteenth and twentieth centuries gave this some continuity. They did, however, as nationalists, question a few generalizations of the colonial historians, but not sufficiently enough so as to change the perspective on Indian society and culture.

Slowly, in the mid-twentieth century, there was a shift in the study of Indian history towards the social sciences. This demanded training in ways of reading a variety of sources, and in learning systems of analyses used in various social sciences as part of methodology. Assessing the validity of a source from more than one perspective was a necessary start; a further step was knowing which methodology could be useful in understanding the nuances of a source. Most non-historians are not aware that history is now a specialized discipline in which the proven reliability of evidence is crucial as a starting point. There is no catechism in historical study—no selected questions and dictated answers. History has to be researched, written and assessed by the trained historian. Historical interpretations may change over time, should there be new proven evidence or new ways of analysing the data that are acceptable to the social sciences, and more so to historians.

Other views of the past are projected in part by the nationalisms of the many segregated groups, each vying for the primacy of its particular identity. These views are questioned by professional historians, and are rejected if they lack the evidence to support what they present. Most non-historians who make pronouncements on history lack training in methods of research, but they nevertheless pronounce upon the past with full confidence, basing themselves either on hearsay or their own imagination. These may be, as they frequently are, those that conform to the Hindutva views on history, given the predominance of Hindu nationalism, but there are others too.

History for them is just a story, a story that I narrate, or you narrate, or anybody else narrates for that matter. Making up stories is great fun and very entertaining as we all know, from having told stories to children and gossiped with adults. But if these stories are claimed as factual, as often happens, then they have to be proved. They cannot be part of entertainment—especially when they become central to the most influential of current storytellers: namely, the media of every kind.

Where nationalism ceases to have the involvement of citizens from across society and is reduced to one majoritarian identity that is given priority, this nationalism denies the essential and substantial components of integrated nationalism, namely, democracy and secularism. Democracy, which is politically crucial to nationalism, is a recognized concept of modern times, as is also secularism—and both are essential to the functioning of the nation-state. Democracy ensures the equality of every citizen and the representation of the views of citizens in governance. Secularism is not just the coexistence of all religions, but rather the establishing of the equal status of all religions and surveillance of religious control over the institutions of a society to ensure that religion is not assumed to be the single most all-powerful concern of the state and society. The historical change brought by nationalism is often sought to be legitimized by insisting on its components having ancestry in antiquity.

In stating that democracy and secularism are essential components of integrated, inclusive nationalism, both terms need some explanation as they are often misunderstood. A democracy is government by the people who elect representatives to do the governing. It does involve the agreement of the majority but this is not a majority constituted by a single identity; those who constitute the majority may well change when the next subject is put to vote. It is neither a majority defined by a single identity, nor does that identity give it permanency. It assumes as fundamental that the people who constitute it are all socially equal and that they come together depending on the subject under consideration, although they may hold different views on other matters. It refers to a system of government that is run by free and independent citizens and governance has also to be in accordance with the will of such people. A pre-selected majority in which the criterion is adherence to a particular identity irrespective of the subject under discussion is therefore not a democratic body.

Secularizing a society is what is meant by secularism and not just opposing religion. Social ethics become the bedrock of a secular society and are established via social justice and the active establishment of the rights of citizens. These are not just targets to be met by bureaucratic ambitions but actions that assist in keeping a society moving forward.

A democratic way of functioning assumes that no category of citizens can have priority over others, irrespective of historical practice or what is projected as cultural heritage or described as the religion of the majority. When historians study past and present religions of the majority over many centuries, two obvious facts emerge. One, that identities are an amalgam of many features;

and two, that they therefore change over time, and each mutation results from new features. A single, unchanging identity does not refer to the same community and their descendants over millennia. The ancestors of those living in the Indian subcontinent today belonged to a range of varied identities from the earliest times. Genetic evidence informs us that the Indian population was a continuing mix of a range of peoples, some that over time became local and some who came from elsewhere.

Secularism underlines democracy by not giving special status to any single religion. It implies that religion is an entirely personal matter and no one is to be discriminated against by the state or society for the religion that a person identifies with. Secularism is not opposition to religion *per se*. In India this would raise the complicated question of which of the sects within a religion would be acceptable to all. Every religion functions through multiple sects not all of which agree about the essentials of belief and worship. This would apply to bigger groups as well. The religion of a tribal community would not be the same as that of the Bhakti teachers. Even Vedic Brahmanism had differences with Puranic Hinduism despite attempts to try and amalgamate the two.

The central issue is that religion should not control civic concerns and institutions. These latter aspects of life should function through a strong ethic that is common to all citizens. A secular society cannot support laws that have the sanction only of one religion. Secularizing a society demands attention to legal orders, freedom of speech, the independence of the individual and the material well-being of the citizen. A society run with a strong ethic does not require religion to order ethical and moral behaviour. Secularism is a marker of historical change with the emergence of a middle class and a nation-state. It is a support for integrated, inclusive nationalism. These broader changes are normal in historical change and should not be taken as a Western imposition on Indian society. It is not a Western pattern as such since it is a change that comes with other features in a society, and more so with what we speak of as modernization.

5

Let me turn now to illustrating what I have said so far on history and nationalism by giving a few examples. The eighteenth-century French Revolution, ushering in aspects of nationalism, claimed some links to ancient Greek democracy. This was to legitimize the change from monarchy to nation-state. Yet there was an absence in Athens of the concepts that set into motion the French Revolution. What was regarded as free citizens constituted a bare fraction of the population of Athens. The overwhelming majority in the Athenian society of the time were slaves and aliens who had no representation or rights in governance. Imbuing governance with an ideal of democracy and taking this back to early centuries was an imaginative way of using the remote past to claim legitimacy for a revolutionary change in eighteenth-century France. The revolution was seeking legitimacy for its call to 'Liberty, Equality and Fraternity' by maintaining that they had existed in ancient times. This is a familiar formulation that continues in our times.

The ideals of the French Revolution in the times of the revolution and subsequent events were beginning to be debated by a wider audience. They were picked up in America and tied into American political thought. As is well established, democracy and representation were discussed with the coming of the nation-state, associated with the emergence of the middle class, with the new technologies and functions of industrialization, and the changes being introduced by capitalism. It entered colonial thinking when these ideas began to be debated in Europe and in the colonies.

The almost unbelievable example of the use of the Greek classics in the discussion of contemporary nationalism and democracy comes from the China of today. The central question is whether the debate on nationalism and democracy in current China can be illumined by re-introducing the study of Greek classical writing on what was regarded as democracy in ancient Greece. The book suggests that the pro- and anti-democracy debate that has hung in the shadows of contemporary China after the Cultural Revolution might be clarified by a reading of the Greek texts. Are contemporary Chinese thinkers imbuing the Greek texts with other meanings, or giving them a different context to use them in supporting the ideas of the Chinese debates?

Some argue that the Indian tradition, since early times, exercised notions of democracy in its forms of governance, even if such a statement has problems finding supportive evidence. Institutions in society emerge when there is historical change and the relevant institutions are required. Democracy means governance by representatives of the people through a method of selection—often an election—and through institutions covering the essentials of governing. Above all, these are answerable to the people to whom they are responsible, and this thinking is of modern times.

Indian sources mention the centrality of the *gana-sangha*s and *gana-rajya*s, especially with reference to oligarchies and chiefdoms. They are more prominent in the Buddhist texts than in the Brahmanical. These are not institutions linked to democracy and they endorse the functioning of clan-based societies in which the dominant clan is pre-eminent. Buddhist institutions suggest a greater familiarity with representing a larger range of views, but this did not mean equality or even representation of all. Seniority was often a qualifier. There is little reflection of the Buddhist ideals in the institutions that had Brahmanical sanction, as is evident from Kautilya's *Arthashastra*.

Free citizens find little mention, nor do instituted methods of representation. It was heads of *kshatriya* families and their kinsmen who more frequently sat in the *sabha* / assembly. The *samiti*s and the *sangha*s / other forms of assemblies may have been a little more broad-based but cannot be described as institutions upholding democracy. These were assemblies more suitable for clan-based societies and chiefships. The *shudra*s and the *dasa*s, despite being the majority, were excluded as they were of low castes. The *panchayat*s of medieval times and the village assemblies such as that of the much-discussed Uttaramerur in Tamil Nadu had a selected membership based on carefully-worked-out formulae guaranteeing that only those selected could be members, and these were invariably members of the upper castes.

Caste society based on *varna,* as described in the *Dharma-shastras,* was a contradiction of democracy. *Varna* referred largely to status in the broader sense and *jati,* the other term, drew from kinship and the closer society, and where hierarchy among these groups was emphasized. The hierarchy conditioned whatever was seen as privileges of status. The search for an established democratic polity in pre-modern India has been unsuccessful. Democracy, essential to a nation-state, came to India later and in modern times, together with unitary nationalism.

Power in early times moved gradually from a larger to a smaller group, crystalizing in one family and one person when kingdoms evolved. The coming of kingdoms may have seen the gradual fading out of clan societies. At the end of the Kurukshetra War, it is said that the *kshatriyas* were destroyed—could this have been a reference to clan-based societies? The argument about the superiority of kingship seems to be encapsulated in the dialogue between Bhishma, lying on a bed of arrows, and Yudhishthira, who was opposed to kingship because he maintained that it involves much violence, as reported in the *Mahabharata.* Bhishma's discourse is a major statement in support of kingship. At the high point of empire, when Kautilya lists the elements that go into the making of the ideal *rashtra* /state, there is no hint of any democratic institution.

6

European social theories of the nineteenth century assessed the colonized as inferior people. The theory of race became prominent and was used, in part, to justify the control of European power over many non-European populations. To legitimize this particular type of control, it seems that the argument of successful conquest was not emphatic enough. The innate inferiority of the dark-skinned colonized people had to be firmly established. Skin colour had a role in ascertaining hierarchy in race. Hence the importance of what came to be called 'race science' in Europe, even if there was little of science in it.

A culture that defined its people as more fair-skinned than another was taken as the superior culture. Thus, the Aryan speakers referring to the *dasas* as dark was interpreted by modern scholars as a reference to skin colour and therefore equated with racial inferiority. By the same token, the Aryan, presumed to be fair, was implicitly superior. The application of race to caste classification further clinched the segregation of the lower castes and the *adivasis* /the first people or, in colonial language, the Scheduled Tribes. The question of whether caste is a form of racial segregation has been debated with some doubt about equating caste with race.

The controversy over the origins of Aryan speakers, for instance, is now largely an argument between professional historians and those with pretensions to knowledge about the 'Aryans'. The theory generally held by scholars is that the initial Aryan speakers migrated from Central Asia in slow stages, whereas the Hindutva theory insists on their homeland being within the boundaries of India. Hindutva holds that both the Hindu and Hinduism originated within India, so they have to argue for indigenous origins. The argument went that for the Hindus, India was both the *pitribhumi* / the land of their ancestors, and the *punyabhumi* / the land of their religion. But defining the boundaries of India— as with land-marked boundaries anywhere—has to contend with the fact of frequent and substantial changes, sometimes within the same century. Even the boundaries of large kingdoms, often referred to as empires, were not permanent, and rarely remained unchanged beyond a century or two, if that. Over a period of four thousand years, the boundaries of India would have changed enormously. The boundaries referred to in the above context were likely those of British India and were not meant to be taken too literally. The imprint of colonial thinking is only too evident in the construction of Hindutva.

The study of the Aryans associated with Vedic texts is a fascinating example of the diverse sources and disciplines that are required in our times for investigating some historical topics, unlike earlier times when the range of sources was more limited and their comprehension less complicated. Thus, in the nineteenth century, a good knowledge of Vedic Sanskrit was sufficient for research, and the entry of other disciplines into this investigation was not anticipated. The focus was on philology. Slowly, however, evidence started coming in from other disciplines. Today the evidence from these multidisciplinary sources has to be correlated with information from the texts.

Challenging information came with archaeological excavations in the early twentieth century, initially unearthing the Indus Civilization and subsequently discovering more associated sites and raising fresh questions on the possible interface of two diverse cultures—the post-Harappan and the Vedic. Archaeological evidence could suggest other leads, such as, for instance, the trade between the Indus region, the Gulf and Mesopotamia. These interactions require extensive excavations and more detailed analyses to clarify the questions now raised in studying cultural history.

Later in the twentieth century came the application of linguistics, necessary to explain the presence of non-Aryan Dravidian linguistic elements in Vedic Sanskrit. Some scholars would also include elements of the Munda languages. These elements are specific only to the oldest Indo-Aryan, as in the Vedic texts, and are absent in the closely related cognate language of Iranian

Aryan, or any other Aryan-based language. This led to asking how and why these elements were incorporated, and what this indicated about the relations between the speakers of the two languages, as suggested by the interpretation of words, phrases and sentences. All this helped to illumine the interface between these different cultures.

In recent years, Aryanism has again become a contention between professional historians and others, although there have been a few exceptions among the latter who are knowledgeable on the subject. The late Iravatham Mahadevan was not a professional historian but was a serious researcher of the early period and observed the methodology of reseach. He did not succeed in deciphering the Harappan script, but in the course of trying to do so, he advanced our understanding of what to look for and how. Initially, the Vedic Aryan culture was said to be foundational to Hinduism. This for Hindutva meant that the Aryans had to have been indigenous, which it interprets as having originated within the boundaries of India. Their religion too, which was taken as the bedrock of Hinduism, had also to have been founded in India.

That the Aryan speakers were indigenous to India has been questioned in the past, on various grounds, and now the questioning comes from a new source of information, this time from geneticists. Their DNA analyses of post-Harappan samples of the second millennium BC shows strains from Central Asian populations.

Historians working on the Vedic period have now to be proficient in understanding genetic data as well, whereas the non-historians writing on the topic can let their fantasies run. Philology has to be correlated with evidence from archaeology, linguistics and genetics—and who knows what evidence other disciplines may contribute next—to both clarify some aspects of the subject and perhaps complicate others. This is just one example of how historians now have to collaborate with specialists in other disciplines as well.

Curiously, little is said these days in the Indian context about the equally viable Aryan culture based in north-eastern Iran, where the Avestan *aryanam* referred to the location of the Aryans. Indo-Aryan and Iranian-Aryan were cognate languages. Many names from the Indian and Iranian-Aryan cultures were similar, but strangely some had diametrically opposite meanings. The words for gods and for demons in the one—*deva* and *asura* in Vedic—were the names for the demons and gods in the other—*daevas* and *ahura* in Avestan. Judging by the names, the relationship was reasonably close but, curiously, practices differed. Advances in knowledge in one discipline can sometimes deeply affect knowledge in another. History is no longer isolated from other related disciplines. Tracing history means being aware not only of its wider reach but also its dialogue with other cultures in neighbouring areas.

The Aryan question that I have touched on, and which is always in the news because of the political controversies it has generated, is currently being much enriched by comparative studies emerging from ideas linked to social and economic anthropology that explain the structure of a variety of societies, or demography that helps explain how population size influences the form of a society, and migrations that are crucial to comprehending the mixture of populations and the resulting cultures.

7

Another foundational view of how history has evolved in the last half century is the increasing centrality of historiography in historical studies. This is a substantial innovation of our times. It involves the analyses of how ideas about the past and theories by which the past is explained are discussed among historians. In other words, how is the past constructed and why does it take the shape it does? This also involves looking at how the historian arrives at an explanation.

Some of these problems are not of the immediate present but have a continuity of a couple of centuries. But earlier they were not recognized as pointers to how history was being written. Colonial writers had argued that Indian civilization lacked a sense of history, since there were no written histories of ancient times as there were among the Greeks, Romans and Chinese. The colonial power, for whom history was the key to understanding the colony they ruled, decided therefore to discover and write the history of the colony. This was done in accordance with the purpose the colonial power had in mind, which, to a lesser degree, was grappling with an unknown past and unfamiliar sources but, to a far greater degree, was intended to strengthen its control over the colony. The past of the Indian colony, if thus constructed, would enable the colonial power to govern the colony the way they wanted to, and, at the same time, claim legitimacy from a version of Indian history that they themselves had constructed. This exercise had obvious advantages for the colonizer. Controlling the course of history through providing a particular past helps to give shape to the present—as is only too well known by many who wish to imprison the past.

Colonial historical scholarship had a basic orientation to the Indian past but it changed when a different reading was required. An initial discovery based on parallels between Sanskrit and Greek suggested some connections obscurely defined. Initially, William Jones, working in Calcutta for the East India Company, studied the *Vedas* and began to see similarities in language and mythology with the Greco-Roman. Some connections could be conceded in the context of their being speakers of Aryan-derived languages. This was not so with other discoveries such as those of James Prinsep, who deciphered the Brahmi script used for writing Sanskrit and Prakrit, which opened up an ocean of inscriptional evidence, distinct from that of the texts. Alexander Cunningham pioneered archaeological excavation providing material evidence of earlier times. The dimension of evidence broadened enormously. But the more purposeful intention of colonial scholarship was to demonstrate that there was an inherent difference in essentials between the European past and the Asian, and that this was made apparent through a distinctly dissimilar history. The suggested similarities of the earliest studies gave way to underlining marked dissimilarities. These dissimilarities insisted on emphasizing the negative aspects of the past of the colony and thus enabled the colonizers to evaluate it as an inferior society.

The Brahmi script having been deciphered, inscriptions could now be read. They provided data on variant aspects of life—kingship, governance, land relations, commerce and aspects of routine living that did not always coincide with the concerns of the texts. The latter were more inclined to concern themselves with matters of belief and worship, although not entirely. Archaeological excavation provided evidence of the distribution of material cultures and the technological practices that characterized cultures. Colonial officers working in India were enthusiastic about these activities, as also were the Indian officials for whom the vision created by this material was new. But the two most influential persons, writing on India in the nineteenth century, worked in England, and both declined to visit India to consult Indian scholars. These two were James Mill and Friedrich Max Müller.

Mill, using his own reflections on what he had read and heard, wrote a history of India. Max Müller made a study of the *Rigveda* and early Vedic texts in their role as the starting point of Indian religion and culture. Their interpretations of the Indian data led to the construction of two images of the Indian past—one dominated the history of the earliest times, and the other of medieval times. Each authored a theory about this past that came to be generally axiomatic about the Indian past. Both of these were prevalent in the nineteenth century and remain popular with the public today.

James Mill wrote the first modern history of India, *The History of British India,* published initially from 1817. Much of it was his personal perspective of Indian history as was to be expected. Mill maintained that this history was that of two nations, the Hindu and the Muslim, quite distinctly separate and constantly in conflict. It is significant that he wrote of two nations but identified them by the two much-mentioned religions. This theory was not questioned and was accepted by other scholars. Indian history was periodized into the earliest Hindu period when Hinduism was powerful, followed by the Muslim period characterized by the domination of Islamic rulers, and finally came the British period as the third, and this was the time of the colonial control of events. This periodization was also accepted without questioning, and deeply coloured the interpretation of Indian history. It has now been questioned in detail and discarded by professional historians. Its single and universally applied explanation of religion as the prime cause of every major historical activity is untenable as a pattern of historical analysis. It continues to be used, however, in popular parlance and thought by many non-historians.

What were the implications of Mill's history? His use of Indian sources was largely minimal. The Hindu period was reconstructed from some reference to Sanskrit texts but used haphazardly since so little was known about this period and the texts at the time when he was writing. The history of what was called the Muslim period drew selectively on Persian sources and largely those linked to the courts of the Sultans and Mughals. The history drawn from these focused on victorious invasions, the glorification of prominent Muslims in contrast to the marginalization of Hindus—the predictable fare of medieval history at that time. Most chronicles of successful invaders in this period were written as eulogies to them and highlighted conquests, especially of rulers newly establishing themselves. The history of the British period was based largely on the records of the East India Company and its activities. English sources at that time had a strong colonial bias.

In inventing this history, the British—in a manner of speaking—reinvented India using their own ways of gathering and interpreting information. Their invention was not intended to encourage the British to settle in India, since this was not their intention anyway, but to make it easier to govern the colony. Unlike the Arabs who came largely as traders and settled in India, and the Turks who initially came as invaders and migrants but also settled in India, the British never settled in India. Furthermore, as compared with the Arabs and the Turks who ploughed back whatever wealth they made into

Indian resources, since these had become their own resources as well, the British did the reverse and took the wealth out of India to Britain. In some cases, they even geared production in India to the demands of British industrialization. For instance, the extensive cultivation of cotton in India was to feed textile mills in Britain. One does not have to keep reiterating 'the drain theory' to demonstrate this. The wealth of India in the precolonial period compared with the poverty of India under colonial rule amply makes the point.

The British version of Indian history, what was in effect their historiography of India, was the kind of history that professional historians saw and see as an attempt to whittle down every cause to a single one—religious difference—and ignore or minimize other causes. The deliberate selection of any single cause and the attempt to give it universal application is anathema to the trained historian. Religion cannot be the sole cause of activities that have a bearing on the making of society and the changes it undergoes, since the construction and functioning of a society is based on far more than merely religious ideas and practices. These latter in themselves are often an attempt to answer the problems faced by a society. This kind of historical writing about India, with a single universally applied explanation for every conflict, was also a travesty of serious history. It was something of a joke when compared with the careful analytical enquiries that British and European historians were making into the European past.

By way of an example, much of European thinking on Asian history initially put the study of Asia into a mould labelled 'Oriental Despotism'. Asian societies were projected as static and registering no change. The cultural pattern was like a pyramid with a highly despotic ruler at the peak controlling all resources through his administration. Those that laboured to produce the wealth, such as peasants, were at the base of the structure and were immersed in poverty. The despot was only concerned with displaying his wealth and living well. Karl Marx's 'Asiatic mode of production' was derived from this mould, as also some ideas of Max Weber and others, especially on the interaction of society and religion.

It was not until the late twentieth century that European and Asian scholars investigating Asian data discovered a different historical reality, and 'Oriental Despotism' was discarded, as was the 'Asiatic mode of production'. This was due to the coming together of various trends in historical analysis. New sources were being discovered with an emphasis on inscriptions and archaeology in the study of the ancient period. New questions were being asked by historians, and among them were some similar to those of the social sciences related to society, economy, religion and cultures. Among these was writing in what has come to be called the Annales School, after the journal by that name published in France, which when translated played a significant initiatory role in introducing the social sciences to

Indian historians; as also did some of the early work of scholars at the University of Chicago; and indeed the ideas of Indian Marxist historians applying the Marxist model and some modified versions of it in historical explanations of the Indian past. Others, inclined towards historiography and interested in the history of ideas, began to investigate the origin and evolution of these, as was being done for various other parts of the world such as in Edward Said's study, *Orientalism*. Change was in the intellectual air and the approach to history participated in this.

8

Mill's two-nation theory had another fallout. It made an impact on politics in colonial India. The veracity of the theory was assumed and was not debated in depth, as it should have been. It became the historical source for projecting two religious nationalisms that were beginning to emerge in the early twentieth century. The theory was thought to provide political and historical legitimacy to these nationalisms. These segregated but conflictual nationalisms based on religious identities differed from the integrated, inclusive, anti-colonial nationalism. The secular democratic nationalism of this latter was central to the movement for Independence. But the two nationalisms qualified by religion—Muslim and Hindu—divided the nation between them. Both argued for the creation of two separate nation-states— the Islamic and the Hindu. The Muslim religious nationalism culminated in the creation of Pakistan, and the Hindu equivalent is intended to convert India into a Hindu Rashtra. The ideologies of religious nationalism were brought to the forefront. Muhammad Ali Jinnah and his colleagues were calling for an Islamic state; Vinayak Damodar Savarkar and his colleagues created the ideology of Hindutva to support a Hindu state.

Ideologies of religious nationalism, both Hindu and Muslim, propagating the two-nation theory of Mill were reinvigorating the colonial concept of India—both of the past and the present. This was not a theory born out of any traditional Indian thinking. It was merely a reconfiguration and endorsement of the British colonial understanding of India. The colonial implant took root, despite India having moved out of colonial control. Having been dismissed officially in the initial period after Independence, the two-nation theory—despite being an inheritance from colonialism—is now being resuscitated, and with disastrous consequences.

As applied in India, in current times, the intention is to eliminate as much as possible of the presence of Islamic culture from the Indian past, so as to reduce or even negate its contribution to the present. Since the presence of an internal enemy is necessary to religious nationalisms, and because they were imprinted with the colonial two-nation theory, the target of hostility for Hindu nationalism was inevitably the Muslim community. It was also regarded as the opponent of the Hindus in the colonial theory of race. The latest move in trying to marginalize the Muslim presence is to substantially change history. The NCERT, or National Council for Educational Research and Training—the body that controls the writing and use of textbooks in government-run and aided schools in India, which are the largest in number—has deleted sections from the official textbooks that cover the syllabus in history. Mughal history has been affected in an effort to cut it down to a minimum to the point of making it redundant. The medieval period in Indian history is generally taken as extending from the thirteenth to the eighteenth centuries AD, of which the Mughal period is from the sixteenth to the eighteenth, and this is the period that is going to be majorly hacked. It is unbelievable that the medieval period will be taught in this truncated fashion.

The non-Muslim activities that were of great consequence in this period will also get deleted since they cannot be taught in a vacuum. As it happens, the sixteenth century was a peak period in the interaction between both Hindu and Muslim cultures as well as in their individual progression. But this will be deleted, as will facets of the Bhakti movement, the literature and compositions in the regional languages, and the great ateliers of miniature painting that had widespread patronage and influence on Indian art. What will happen to the many remarkable buildings of the medieval period located all over the country whose architectural traits come from a variety of sources? One dare not ask. This kind of treatment of the discipline of history can only be viewed as the activity of those who know virtually nothing about history in general nor the actual history of the second millennium AD in particular.

From the historical perspective, we may well ask whether the dual division projected by religious nationalism had and has evidence to support it. More often than not, the required evidence for such theories was either barely marginal or absent. In this, it is held that a major cause for the separation of the two communities was that the Hindus were heavily victimized by the Muslims after the start of Muslim rule. This victimization has to be avenged, now that the Hindus are in a position to do so. The supposedly irrefutable evidence of the division was that the Muslims who ruled during the last thousand years treated the Hindus as enslaved people. This has now become a political slogan of Hindu religious nationalism in dislodging a particular community and supposedly seeking revenge. The image projected is that of the unfailing violence and aggression of the Muslim against the Hindu. The professional activity of the Hindus was either terminated or reduced to a minimum. They were socially ostracized and, above all, forcibly converted to Islam. As non-Muslims, they also had to pay a tax, the *jaziya*. Those who should know better are ready to propagate this theory without asking any questions about its veracity.

The blanket or umbrella terms 'Hindu' and 'Muslim' were used to cover any group that might even vaguely be linked to either of these religious identities. Attempts to examine the constituents of these terms were not made in any detail, nor the observation of differences within each. 'Muslim', for instance, was taken as a unified, single category, whereas actually there were marked differences between Sunnis and Shias, not to mention other sects labelled as Muslim, such as Khojas and Dawoodis (or Ismaili Khojas and Dawoodi Bohras).

Similarly, those that were bracketed as Hindus would have defined themselves more precisely as belonging to one among the various sects of Vaishnavas, Shaivas and Shaktas or some other group. Had modern scholars used the Persian, Sanskrit and Indian regional-language sources more analytically, they would have noticed the multiple sects of both religions, since these sources did not use the blanket terms to any degree until the last few centuries. Clarity about these perceptions makes a difference in how groups of people in a society view each other.

The use of the label Muslim in Indian languages was infrequent in earlier times. The references were more often to Yavanas and Tajiks for the Arabs or those coming from the West. Yavana was a back-formation from the Iranian *yauna* and related to the Prakrit *yona*, all referring to the ancient Greeks who also came to India from the western direction. The label of Shakas went back to those who had invaded and migrated from Central Asia at the turn of the Christian era. It was now used for those who came from the same places in Central Asia and migrated to India where they settled. The term Turushkas, used initially for the Central Asian Turks, came to be applied later and more extensively to mean Muslims who had settled in India. Kalhana, for instance, writing in the twelfth century, refers to the Kushans, who were earlier by a millennium, as Turushkas. He thus gives them a contemporary label, since they came from the same region although they were not Turks, and Islam was non-existent in the time of the Kushans. Sometimes such persons were referred to by their clan names. Such clan names could become caste names, and among them, some were used by both Hindu and Muslim castes. The identity, therefore, was primarily geographical and ethnic, not religious. The change to a religious identity occurred later and the reasons for this have yet to be fully explored.

Every religion does not express itself or organize itself in an identical way in its practice. India had its own unique way of doing so, which seems to have been picked up by the more popular religions. The articulation of Islam, as also with Hinduism, is more in the form of various smaller groups, sects and cults that may have an overall reference to Islam but whose religion is more closely defined by the sect they identify with. This is characteristic of virtually every religion in India. It is difficult, therefore, to assume that some event that triggers off an action in a particular Islamic sect or group will be repeated in another such group not closely connected with the first. The overarching formulation of a religion in India to cover the range of diverse sects as a single religion is a relatively modern phenomenon. Was the evolution of a religion, when practised in India, influenced by the Indian social context, such that its articulation took a form different from that in other major cultures? It has been argued that there is some difference between the Islamic communities that evolved in India from Arab connections as compared with those from Central Asian connections.

Politicians with a certain view and others who should know better are again endorsing the historically now-defunct two-nation theory. In recent times it is receiving attention in some circles. Professional historians have questioned, and are questioning, the very basis of this theory. There is far more information on this period of history now, and the historical sources are being researched carefully by historians. When these sources are read in historical context, they read differently and tell a different story from the popular versions. They do not rejuvenate the view of colonial historians.

9

The dictionary tells us that to victimize is to make a victim of a person or a specific group of people by cheating, swindling and defrauding them, or denying them any freedom, or slaughtering them in the manner of a sacrificial victim. Victimization is not unknown to most premodern societies in many parts of the world. Those having access to power and wealth did not always refrain from humiliating and harming those without. In India, upper-caste Hindus have been familiar with this social condition and with the accompanying attitudes and activities for more than two millennia, well before Islam came into existence. Some endorsed it as the right of the upper castes; others endorsed it perhaps unthinkingly by not opposing it and allowing it to be observed; and some did speak up against it—but their minority view did not result in its termination or its wider questioning.

Those referred to in our times as Dalits, the lower castes and untouchables, have been excluded, ghettoized and discriminated against by the upper castes for some two millennia. It was claimed that their touch was polluting. They were placed in a separate category of those without or outside caste, labelled the *avarna*, in contrast to those who belonged to a caste, *savarna*. The theory of their being impure humans permitted the pure ones to treat them in any way they wished, even brutally and harmfully, or make them do the worst of jobs. They lived in separate parts of the village or town and were denied water from the common well and entry to the temple sanctum. The sharp distinction between *savarna* and *avarna* hardened the demarcation and stymied social concern. The basic concept of holding every human as being equal and the freedom to assert this were denied to them. This in itself annulled the application of notions of equality and freedom in social behaviour. Civilizations generally did not assume social equality in their societies, so in this India was not different. But what made the Indian condition worse was the insistence that these humans, the lowest of the low, were impure human beings and therefore untouchable. This situation is affirmed in texts that date to what is described as the 'golden age' of the Indian past.

These extreme forms of discrimination, more consistently observed by upper-caste Hindus, were denied in theory by other religions in India, but this did not stop them from observing discrimination in practice. Even on conversion to other religions, and especially those that proclaimed the equality of all, this social distancing was nevertheless maintained. As a category across religions, those thus outcasted may well have constituted the largest in number. It would have included the Hindu *avarna*s, Muslim *pasmanda*s, and later Sikh *mazhabi*s, Christian Dalits, and suchlike, although the rule about untouchability may have been a trifle more muted among some. Dalit Muslims in Bihar and Uttar Pradesh, who worked as sweepers and cleaners, often referred to as Halalkhors and Lal Begis, continue to be segregated. Yet Islam and Christianity are religions that formally hold all of mankind to have been created equal.

The practice of large sections of society being excluded and victimized was prevalent among all those of higher status. Many questions therefore arise that are fundamentally important to our society. Were practices of this kind directed less at particular religious communities and more at the *avarna*s? Are these practices that essentially involve lower levels of society defined more by caste than by other identities, or do they change with purpose and intention? Significantly, in Sanskrit and in Indian regional-language sources, Muslims are generally not referred to as Muslim but by ethnic or alternative labels. Or the term *mleccha* is used, which had a broad reach and included those thought of as alien or of low status. The significance of this to the worldview of Indian society has yet to be analysed. Many questions arise that are central to social history.

An awareness of the historical context within which we speak of victimization is crucial in recognizing that it was a form of action and behaviour that existed in India over the last two millennia. That the victimization was justified by caste differences does not exonerate those that victimized the lesser castes, irrespective of who they were. A high degree of aggression would also apply to those who victimized others on the basis of religious identities. Whereas there is evidence of all kinds, such as the curtailing of upward social mobility and the enforcing of demeaning practices, which make clear that the victimization of the *avarnas* was practised and accepted across Indian society, however, in the case of religious hostility, there would be aggression and conflict, but victimization would require an ordering of society as in the case of the *avarnas*.

The characteristics of victimization are clear. Those victimized have to live segregated in ghettoes beyond the normal boundaries of village and town; their access to employment is extremely limited and what is open to such groups is of the most demeaning kind; they have to carry marks to identify themselves; and they are socially ostracized.

To posit caste identities or the lack thereof as important causes of physical aggression is not to suggest that there was no history of religious conflict in India prior to the coming of 'Muslim' rule. I have already given examples of ongoing religious conflict. We characterize our civilization as always having been tolerant and non-violent, but even if there were no fierce large-scale religious wars, as were witnessed in some other parts of the world, there are nevertheless manifestations of violent religious intolerance. Much of this focused on dissenting ideas and these, as essential characteristics of all civilizations, add to the intellectual dimensions of religious and secular thinking. Such ideas encourage doubt, questioning and debate. They are highly valued in philosophical enterprise as they involve a variety of knowledge systems, as is evident, for instance, in Nyaya philosophy and as brought into play in Charvaka thinking. But apart from these, all advanced cultures such as the Indian also indulge in the politics of power and social control. Ideas contradictory to those of the orthodoxy are sought to be tackled in various ways.

10

Hinduism was projected as a monolithic and unified religion in recent centuries, possibly to bring it into alignment with the dominant Abrahamic religions. Yet when examined as a practice, it appears to be more of a clustering of diverse sects. Some had common ideas and just a few differences; others had differing degrees of belief and ritual—some closely related and some distant. This is what gives it an enviable flexibility and a richness that comes from appropriating and internalizing beliefs, and articulating these in their diverse forms in the course of its history. Where these beliefs and practices remain pristine and not obfuscated by ritual—admittedly difficult to define and locate—there the religion is one of much subtlety. This may well be found more at the philosophical level than in the rituals of worship. Much of the dissenting tradition was an attempt to nourish and protect the diversity of the teachings.

However, as in every organized religion the world over, there are sociopolitical and economic demands made on the religion, especially by the powerful in society, through diverse forms of patronage and its social articulation. These evolve through the centuries. They lead to distancing the religion. It takes variant forms that comply with the views of the controlling institutions. This is done by trying to silence dissent or the critiques of these institutions. Thus, for those whose religious beliefs differed but who were nevertheless competing for a following, dissenting groups were not to be accommodated. Their teachings were negated, often in nonviolent ways but sometimes even in violent ways, such that it is difficult to maintain that any society from pre-modern times was always tolerant and nonviolent. Violent methods of silencing could take the form of victimization.

Victimization by certain social groups of other groups is present in most societies and can be marginally present in what we label as civilizations. Outstanding intellectual and artistic achievements require a reasonably smooth-running society. In early times, such societies were built on the easy supply of and control over labour and resources. Access to these often required coercing those that provided such necessities, coercion that would be more successful if couched in terms of necessary and established social norms. Victimization as an extreme form of coercion required an excuse to justify it. It also enhanced, and continues to do so, the notion of persecution, although the social parameters of this may differ.

Persecution affects many social parameters, and in the Indian context it sometimes drew on caste norms or else resulted from what is usual in most societies—political confrontations, status differences, social origins, gradually including hostility from differences in belief and forms of worship. The evidence is at the moment scattered. It needs to be systematically brought together and properly studied.

Dissenting ideas of a religious nature became only too apparent as part of the intellectual challenges to Vedic Brahmanism in the first millennium BC. Buddhists and Jainas were referred to as *shramanas*, so named from the term used for monks—*shramana*—who laboured to achieve *nirvana* /enlightenment. To these were added other groups such as the Ajivikas and the Charvakas, whose teachings also did not conform to Brahmanism. All of them, as a collective, were opposed to the basic beliefs of Vedic Brahmanism as they did not accept the existence of deities, questioned the sacrality of the *Vedas* and doubted rebirth in the form as taught by the *brahmanas*. Vedic Brahmanism declared those that disagreed as *nastikas* / non-believers in deity, as they also did even in later times when referring to those that did not accept the Puranic deities.

That the dissenting views between various religious sects in the mid-first millennium BC could become confrontational is evident in the edicts of Ashoka Maurya. He states that there should be tolerance not only between *brahmanas* and *shramanas* but among all sects. Clearly, differences of opinion were not just passing doubts and debating items but had a serious presence in society. The much-respected grammarian of Sanskrit of that time, Patanjali, comes up with a telling image when he compares the relationship between the *brahmanas* and the *shramanas* to that between the snake and the mongoose.

There are repeated references in Buddhist texts, from the early *Divyavadana* to the later *Manjushri-mula-kalpa*, stating that the one who usurped the Mauryan throne, Pushyamitra, thereby founding the Shunga dynasty, destroyed Buddhist monasteries and *stupa*s, burnt their libraries and killed Buddhist monks. This is repeated in Chinese and Tibetan Buddhist texts of the latter part of the first millennium AD. Inscriptions mention the *ashvamedha*s / elaborate Vedic horse sacrifices that Pushyamitra conducted, which would point to his being a patron of Vedic Brahmanism and therefore opposed to Buddhism.

There were multiple texts and sects following the teachings of varied teachers whom we include in the label of Hinduism. Many of these were introducing new ideas and forms of worship. The most influential of these were the Shaiva and the Vaishnava sects focusing on new forms of worshipping the two deities—Shiva and Vishnu. The incorporation of the Shakta cults gave them a strong presence, especially in the latter part of the first millennium AD. There was occasional hostility among these sects but not of much consequence. Religious conflict seems to have been more common between the Shaivas and the *shramanas*. Apart from the Ashokan edicts, texts in Sanskrit, Chinese, Tibetan and Persian of the first two millennia AD provide relevant information.

The detailed account of the travels of the seventh-century Chinese Buddhist pilgrim Xuanzang, who journeyed widely overland, and finally stayed for some years in the monastery at Nalanda, refers to inter-religious relations. He mentions the persecution of Buddhists through the destruction of monasteries and the killing of monks at various times. He also mentions the violent acts of the king Shashanka of eastern India who was known to be hostile to Buddhists.

The historian of Kashmir, Kalhana, writing his history of Kashmir, the *Rajatarangini*, in the early twelfth century, is contemptuous of the *brahmanas* of the Gandhara region in the north-west of the subcontinent because, as he explains, they accepted land grants from those Shaiva kings who oversaw the killing of Buddhist monks. Kalhana also records the frequency with which Hindu kings of the late first millennium AD looted the considerable wealth of Hindu temples. When there was a fiscal crisis in Kashmir during the reign of the king Harshadeva, in the eleventh century AD, the king appointed officers, specially designated to supervise the looting, and he gave them the title of *devotpatana-nayaka*—officer in charge of uprooting the gods—indeed an ironic title.

The wealth of the Buddhists made them prominent as recipients of patronage, and this, combined with their teachings, gave them enormous followings. This allowed them to build substantial *viharas* / monastic centres, *chaityas* / places of worship, and *stupas* / mounds for burying relics. But gradually, the Jaina monks were also attacked when they began to receive impressive donations and, similar to the earlier Buddhists, attracted large followings. These attacks are sometimes associated with the competition to convert the king. The Jainas were settled in large numbers in Gujarat and in parts of Karnataka and Tamil Nadu. It is from these areas that come inscriptions referring to their persecution.

Impressionistically at least, the Shaivas seem to have been active in the conflict, but this would need to be investigated. The seventh-century Pallava king Mahendravarman is said to have impaled 8,000 Jaina monks for threatening to kill a Shaiva teacher. The figure of the impaled monks does not speak well for the king's ethics, but ethics are often set aside in such conflicts. It is unclear whether there was a genuine threat of a major kind to the Shaivas, or whether the king having just been converted from Jainism to Shaivism wished to demonstrate his ardour for his new religion. Such arguments and the numbers quoted seem exaggerated. A thirteenth-century inscription at Ablur in Dharwad records the construction of a Shaiva temple over the ruins of a Jaina temple destroyed by Shaivas. The destruction of Jaina temples and the building of Shaiva temples on the ruins is mentioned elsewhere as well. Yet, soon after this, in the second millennium AD, the most impressive Jaina temples were constructed. Clearly, the Jainas had both patronage and an effective following. By the sixteenth century, the Jaina religion was markedly present and represented in the gatherings on religious discourse initiated by Akbar.

Of the two significant *shramana* religions—Buddhism and Jainism—the latter flourished in the second millennium AD. This may well have been due to its arduous rituals and activities, of which many were linked to commerce within the subcontinent. The wealth associated with the Jainas is mentioned in the sources and is exhibited in their extensive and highly decorated temple architecture, what might be called the Indian rococo and is an indication of their economic success and social prestige.

The Buddhists were also targeted in conflicts between the Chalukyas and the Rashtrakutas when Buddhist *chaitya* halls were converted into temples, and the image of the Buddha was replaced by that of a Hindu deity. There are, of course, varying historical reasons for these religious conflicts. Buddhism was gradually ousted and replaced by Puranic Hinduism. Many reasons have been suggested. Royal patronage declined as did donations from the wealthy. Places of worship were being built for Hindu deities. Many grants of land were given to *brahmanas*. The observation of caste rules seems to have become more regular, or at least the formal obeisance to them.

Buddhism moved to eastern India and had close contact with Tibetan Buddhism. Its decline in India was in part because some practices and beliefs were appropriated by Hindu practices and ideas. The worship of icons was one such. Other reasons had to do with both changes within the religion and a turnover of patrons. However, its decline in India was far outweighed by its becoming the predominant religion in South-East and Central Asia and in many parts of East Asia. This may well have been tied to the dramatic expansion of maritime trade in the Indian Ocean and land-based exchanges in Central Asia. Buddhism travelled with the trade, not only through the missionary monks who journeyed alongside the traders but also because the religious institutions were participants in the trade.

11

Other aspects of Hinduism evolved in various ways and became prominent. The label of Puranic Hinduism, among others, incorporates these. Hinduism gave prominence to particular deities such as Vishnu, Shiva and Durga, and later inducted Shakta worship and rituals. The popularity of worshipping these deities both in themselves and in a variety of their incarnated forms led to large followings and donations. Unlike Vedic Brahmanism, this form of the religion opened up to many social levels. Both the building of temples as sacred spaces and the icons housed in these spaces for worship were new features, although already in use by the *shramana* religions. The composition of extensive texts, the *Puranas*, on aspects of Puranic Hinduism, was also undertaken in these times. The popularity of Puranic Hinduism can be attributed in part to its induction of popular rituals and beliefs into an expanding universe of deities and events. Whereas Vedic Brahmanism was highly exclusive and almost fenced in with its dialogue extending largely to the upper castes, Puranic Hinduism, although it had an exclusive segment, was more open to incorporating popular manifestations of belief and worship and adding to its pantheon of deities.

Another new form in the evolution of the Hindu religion also had a far-reaching effect. This was the growth of what has come to be called Bhakti, a form of worship consisting largely of expressing personal devotion to a chosen deity. The Bhakti Movement began in South India but the articulation also took form in various parts of the northern subcontinent in the second millennium AD. By the latter part of this millennium, it had many centres in the subcontinent, not identical but sharing some similarities. The deity could be worshipped in the abstract, although iconic forms became popular. Intermediaries and priests were not required, nor a formulaic ritual of worship, but, needless to say, both these did intervene in those Bhakti sects that became established. Hymns and songs were composed by followers in the course of worship and the practice of the religion. That it may have borrowed from Shramanic thought and rituals is an opinion that has been expressed but not sufficiently discussed.

The older forms continued, but many new religious expressions and new presentations of the chosen deities became popular, with some being introduced into the texts and teachings. What is so striking is that this trend was being taught, discussed and practised, precisely in the period of 'Muslim' rule, the second millennium AD, throughout much of the subcontinent. The cultures of these religious traditions saw the striking growth of many facets of Puranic Hinduism, the highlight being from the fifteenth to the seventeenth century and thus coinciding with Mughal rule.

Bhakti centres developed their own subdivisions largely tied to the local language and religious traditions, and the result was again the growth of many sects around each. Devotion to deity was required and the bestowal of grace from the god was desired. Neither the deity nor its incarnation, nor the specific forms of belief and worship, were identical. Devotion to a single deity did not preclude understanding the meaning of worship on a larger scale—who does one worship and why—as also the emphasis on the ethics of social actions. Religious teachings were not limited to those of one faith as ideas could be picked up from many sources.

One of the characteristics of Bhakti teaching was that it was open to everyone, and the devotees of Bhakti *sant*s / holy men, were from any and every religious background. Hindus and Muslims comfortably worshipped the same deity and followed the same teacher. Thus, Kabir was a Muslim weaver but also a follower of Ramananda the Vaishnava teacher. Similarly, Ras Khan was the son of a Muslim landowner but was an ardent Krishna-*bhakt* / worshipper of Krishna.

Among the arrivals from Central Asia into northern India who had a significant impact were the Sufis, bringing with them the teachings of their diverse sects. This was an activity introducing new ideas and they set up centres with the patronage of both the sultans and the local people. As with such religious movements, there were two developments in their establishing themselves. One was royal patronage which did, however, involve some of them with the politics of the court. The other was the more important, the emphasis on popular support. That their coming coincided with the spread of the Bhakti teachers just might have made the Sufis as religious groups more accessible. Some Sufi teachers supported the Islamic orthodoxy but the larger number were free in their thought and encouraged dialogue with those of other religions. The dialogue between the Nath yogis and the Sufis settled in Punjab is an impressive example. Places where the Sufis lived and taught had audiences and followers of both the major religions and many others. Pursuing these dialogues would tell us more about popular religious ideas of that time.

It is evident that the Mughal period, from the sixteenth to the eighteenth century, was one of the more creative periods in Indian history. There was a remarkable cultural synthesis in aesthetics. There was immense intellectual curiosity and much exchange of ideas in many kinds of studies written in Sanskrit and Persian. Above all, it was a time when the multiple sects of Hinduism and Islam expressed religion in forms either subtle or clearly manifested, and often in ways that were new in the use of words. These remain part of the lives of many Indians to this day.

12

Since so much of crucial importance is imputed as resulting from religious antagonism and victimization, it would be worth looking at some recorded instances of contacts and practices in the relations involving the two communities, the Hindu and the Muslim, and in the period of the last thousand years when they were living together in the subcontinent. Such a survey would help to assess whether victimization was at the root of these relations. Sometimes the statements that are made about Hindu–Muslim relations are incorrect because the sources have not been consulted, or else they have not been understood correctly. At other times there is little or no awareness of the sources and the statements come from non-historians indulging in an ideology that has, on occasion, become a fantasy. I would like to give a few examples of situations involving both communities as indicators of what was a sizeable part of the relationship between the two.

A popular belief is the explanation often given for the ritual of becoming a *sati*. A recently widowed woman has to immolate herself together with her dead husband when he is placed on the funeral pyre. It is said that the custom became necessary after the Muslim invasions began in the second millennium AD, because the invaders grossly misbehaved with the conquered population, especially the women. Apart from the fact that such an argument exonerates the society from having to ensure the protection of all, the ritual itself is an inexcusable attempt to shake off responsibility and allow a despicable treatment of women to be hallowed by calling it a ritual. Historically, it is an error. There are references to the immolation of widows in various texts of the earlier, pre-Islamic period. None of them are explained as being necessary because of the fear of what invaders do to women, and there was no shortage of invaders in previous centuries.

The *Rigveda* hints at the ritual but with a difference, stating that a woman should lie with her dead husband on the funeral pyre but should leave the pyre before it is lit. There is a debate in the relevant section of the *Mahabharata* on whether or not Madri should immolate herself on the death of Pandu. There is a difference of opinion in the two seventh-century AD texts of Banabhatta: the occurrence of *sati* is described in his *Harshacharita*, but there is opposition to it in his *Kadambari*. The more firmly recorded evidence comes from the Eran inscription of AD *c*.510, inscribed during the rule of a Gupta king. It is stated that Goparaja, a person of high status, having died in battle, his wife decided on becoming a *sati* and the inscription is a record of this act.

There are other early forms in which a woman becoming a *sati* is commemorated, as in stone engravings and plaques located in various places, each carrying specific symbols associated only with commemorating women who became *satis*. Generally, such a memorial is just a stone slab on which is carved the right arm of a woman with her bangles intact. A widow had to break her bangles on her husband's death, but by becoming a *sati* she continued to live together with her husband in their life after death. Such memorials, in pre-Islamic times, are few in number and are found in specific locations. More elaborate *sati* memorials and even very small *sati* temples are known from much later times and in limited locations.

The popularity of the ritual also varies. Stone slabs recording *sati* memorials have their own distinctive symbols, as do the hero-stones—going back to the early first millennium AD—commemorating those who died defending the village cattle in a cattle raid or died in battle. Initially, these were memorials treated as somewhat apart from formal religion. Hero-stones illustrate the idea of the hero being taken up to heaven, often by the *apsaras* / celestial maidens. Rebirth is not for these heroes. (This in itself could be taken as a comment on the theory of *karma*.) Gradually, but only marginally, these rituals came to be incorporated in the formal religion. In medieval times there are more memorials to heroes and *satis*, often described as *kirti-stambhas* / pillars of fame, literally. Hefty battles were fought in many parts of the subcontinent but *sati* memorials are not to be found in every area linked to battles. Judging by the hero-stone memorials, cattle raids were the more frequent cause of a hero's death. A count of the various categories of memorials would give a better explanation for the performance of the ritual.

In modern times there developed a certain embarrassment at this grotesque demand on women, even if it was not enforced on a large scale. However much a woman becoming a *sati* might be venerated, it was fundamentally an imprint of the inferiority of a woman's life that she was required to sacrifice it when her husband died. An attempt to provide a justification, one that continues to be repeated despite evidence to the contrary, is that it had come into practice subsequent to the Muslim invasions since the women captured were manhandled in horrific ways. This was part of the argument of ceaseless conflict between the two religious communities and of the victimization of Hindus by Muslims, an explanation rejected by historians.

The historical evidence is clear that the ritual of becoming a *sati* dates to well before Islam was even thought of, leave alone the invasion of Muslim armies. As a ritual, *sati* was not unknown in early times, although obviously it was not invariably performed. We have to explain why *sati* has been resorted to on some occasions even though its practice has been a subject of debate. Was it required from women of all social strata or only from those of higher status? Why does the woman have to be ritually sacrificed to attain social upgradation? It has also been suggested that it might have had its origins in the need to overcome possible contentions over succession and inheritance of property. Explanations have to be more searching for this unsupportable requirement from women.

13

Turning to the relations between members of the two communities, these cannot be discussed as a single conglomerate since they are expressed in different ways at diverse social levels. It might be clearer to look at the evidence from various sources not by the languages that they are written in but by the social group that they are describing. The varieties of sources also require more exposure. Inscriptions from the twelfth century AD onwards, for example, have not been sufficiently consulted when historical questions are being debated. Yet they often provide precise and reliable evidence, especially on social history.

I would like to consider the broader relations between Hindus and Muslims during the second millennium AD, in other words over the last thousand years, when Hindus are said to have been victimized by Muslims. My examples are taken at random, revealing conditions at various levels of society, in order to attempt a generalized view. The evidence is culled from a variety of sources, largely in Sanskrit and in the regional languages and authored by non-Muslims—those that are said to have been victimized. These voices have not been heard as often as they should have been. Nor has enough attention been given to their perspective on the relationship between Hindus and Muslims as expressed in the terms that they used for each other and the context of these.

Starting at the level of the elite, we know that quite a few Hindu royal families continued to be regarded as being of high social status. This was one reason why some sultans and Mughal rulers married into these families. The rajas who accepted suzerainty and were inducted into the administration often enough remained at the head of the administration in their erstwhile kingdoms and were given the continuing status and title of *raja*, sometimes together with a *mansab* / an administrative rank not without some income. The politics of administration would have benefitted from some continuation of the existing system. Such rajas' income—agrarian and commercial—was sufficient for maintaining their aristocratic style of living.

There was a scatter of rajas across the Mughal domains. Some who had held the title of *maharajadhiraja* also took the title of *suratrana* / the adaptation of sultan. One Vijayanagara raja adopted the title of *hinduraya-suratrana* / the Hindu king the sultan, taking no chances! The ambiguity is, however, whether by *hindu* he was referring to a person from the geographical entity al-Hind or to the religion—of being a Hindu—since both meanings were current. Earlier titles such as *ranaka, rauta, thakkura* and *nayaka* were not necessarily given up. Some Hindu officers at a high level of administration continued their work and were also collectors of revenue for the administration. Where this was a family occupation, as it often was, they knew what the work entailed. Inscriptional records, if written in Sanskrit as many were, had *brahmana* authors, and it always helps when there is a continuity in the records. Many more records and royal orders were in the form of *firmans*. Local-level administration appears to have had some degree of continuity from pre-Islamic times.

14

Appointing local persons to high office was a practice that went back centuries, providing as it did a closer control over local matters by the central administration. This may well be a reason for Turkish, Afghan and Mughal rulers—the 'Muslims' as we call them, or 'Turushkas' as they were then called—appointing Rajputs to high office, or retaining them. The Mughal economy, for instance, was in the trusted hands of Raja Todar Mal. Another Rajput, Raja Man Singh of Amber, commanded the Mughal army at the Battle of Haldighati. He defeated the Rajput against whom the battle was being fought, Maharana Pratap, who was an opponent of the Mughals. Pratap's army had an effectively large contingent of Afghan soldiers led by Hakim Khan Suri, a descendant of Sher Shah Suri. If seen purely in terms of religion, this could be described as a noticeable Muslim contingent in an army that included a Muslim commander, fighting in support of a Rajput Hindu.

But battles, as we know, are often occasions for sorting out not just one confrontation but a variety of conflictual and uncertain relations. Some antagonisms were caused primarily because kingdoms had been lost to the new conquerors and these were sought to be regained. Other hostilities arose from a variety of conflicts that come to the fore on such occasions. The Kacchwaha Rajputs, who were close to the Mughals, were leading the Mughal army. They were also settling scores with the Sisodia Rajputs, one of whom was Maharana Pratap. So they were fighting on opposite sides. A considerable degree of antagonism in this situation can be attributed to conflicts over regaining kingdoms lost to the new conquerors. This would be one motivation for both Maharana Pratap and Hakim Khan Suri to oppose the Mughals. Clearly there was far more involved in the conflict than just a Hindu resistance to Muslim rule.

Both political and religious identities had participants on each side in a complex political conflict. Rajput clans had differing loyalties among themselves and towards the imperial power. It might be more correct to say that the political reading of the battle is that it was an event in which a Rajput allied with an Afghan were both battling for what they perceived as their patrimony, taken from them by Mughal rule. One may think again about the primary causes of this battle and reconsider whether religious conflict was the chief cause of the hostility.

Hindus working in the Mughal administration in high offices were mainly from the upper castes— *brahmanas, kayasthas, khattris*. Well-established Jainas are also mentioned. This was virtually a continuation of the earlier system of the higher administration being in the hands of the upper castes. It made sense to use the earlier administrators since these were the persons who would have both the experience and the understanding of handling administrative problems. We learn much from the writings of Chandra Bhan, who held the highest offices in the court of Aurangzeb and had also served Jahangir and Shah Jahan in his earlier days. He recorded his comments on their activities in his writings, and more fully on the last of these three emperors. He made a point of reiterating that he was a *brahmana* and a practising Hindu. His scholarship in Persian was on par with his scholarship in Sanskrit and was much praised by the knowledgeable members of the imperial court. He mentioned other upper-caste Hindu ministers in Mughal service suggesting some continuation of the pattern.

Interestingly, when narrating the history of India going back to the time of the *Mahabharata*, Chandra Bhan emphasized the role of Yudhishthira in the events he thought of as significant. He narrated in greater detail the activities of Rajput rulers as well as the various sultans, coming up to the Mughals. His incorporation of the Mughal genealogy into this narrative has been commented upon and explained as perhaps being an attempt to bring them into the formal historical narrative. The use of the past to give legitimacy to the present was not an unknown practice, whether among scholars of Persian or of Sanskrit.

The intervention of Hindu rajas in the politics of the Mughal court was in some instances substantial. One example that went on for more than a generation was that of Mughal relations with Bundelkhand. The Bundela raja, Bir Singh Deo, who was close to Jahangir and held one of the highest Mughal *mansab*s / ranks and revenue assignment, was so embroiled in Mughal court politics that he was linked to the assassination of Abul Fazl, the chief chronicler and close friend of Akbar. This was not the expression of a Hindu–Muslim conflict. It had deeper ramifications involving the struggle for succession within the Mughal royal family, the variant factions at the Mughal court and their aspirations, and the attempt of a lesser Rajput to muscle into the highest level of politics at the royal court directly involving the royal family.

15

Among the more impressive symbols of political power, dating back to much earlier times and used by various rulers in past centuries, were immensely large inscribed pillars. The Mauryan emperor Ashoka set up pillars in the heart of his empire, the inscriptions on which reflected his ideas on governance and some of his policies, apart from his thoughts that might have arisen from his interest in Buddhism. It was a way of directly communicating with his subjects. Later rulers, wishing to associate with the past of the country that they ruled over, could either add their message or relocate the pillar to a more striking current location. This may have been a gesture of borrowing the glory of their predecessors or asserting their own success.

These were not specific connections with the past because by now it would seem that none could read the script of the earlier inscriptions, nor did they know who the authors were. What then was the meaning of this relocation of pillars? Was it celebrating their own victory as sultans, or was it a link to the history of earlier times, or something of both? Much care was taken to ensure that the pillars were not damaged or destroyed. Even though immensely difficult to transport, as is clear from the description of how this was done, the pillars were nevertheless carried over long distances and relocated with pride in new places of importance and treated with respect by those in power.

An early relocation in the second millennium AD was undertaken by Iltutmish who brought the iron pillar of the mid-first millennium AD to Delhi. The design of the pillar evokes the earlier Ashokan pillars with its faintly tapering shaft, and an elongated carved abacus that may possibly have had an animal capital, and an inscription mentioning a deity. The inscription on the shaft is in the Gupta-period Brahmi script and states that it was erected by a king called Chandra. The script could not be read by the early second millennium AD, but we can now read it thanks to the nineteenth-century decipherment of the Brahmi script. The identity of Chandra is not certain but he could have been Chandragupta II of the Gupta dynasty.

The original location of the pillar is uncertain but it may have come from the city of Udayagiri near Vidisha, Madhya Pradesh, and transported by Sultan Iltutmish. Variations on this narrative mention other rulers. It appears to be a victory monument which invokes the god Vishnu. There is an additional small inscription on the pillar that records the settling of Delhi by the Tomar ruler Anangpal in 1109 AD. Delhi was held by the Tomars and the Chahamanas before it was conquered by the Turushkas. The iron pillar may well have been treated as a symbol of victory, and therefore erected prominently in the courtyard of the mosque. Yet the symbol was effectively a Hindu one. No attempt was made to convert it into an Islamic symbol.

A later sultan, Feroz Shah Tughlaq, referred to as Peroj Sahi in the Hindi inscriptions, was greatly interested in the pillars from past times and wanted to know who had erected them and what was engraved on them. He was disappointed that the texts could no longer be read, even by learned *brahmanas*. He was not convinced by the exaggerated stories he was told about the pillars being the staffs of the hero Bhima in ancient times. It might be interesting to speculate that if the inscriptions could have been read in those times, then what would have been the subject of discussion at the court of the Tughlaq sultans on the statements of Ashoka, and more so in the context of the subsequent history of two millennia. There would surely have been an invigorating debate.

Feroz Shah had the pillars transported with much effort and organization to various important locations at considerable distances. One was placed like a surrogate crown, firmly on top of his citadel at Kotla in Delhi, where it still stands, and could once be seen for miles around. Apart from his curiosity about what was written on the pillars, was Feroz Shah anxious to have a link with the past, and was this in part because his mother was a Bhatti Rajput from Punjab? Or was he interested in displaying a stunning historical object that would draw attention to him as well when he moved it to the new location? Among those that visit Kotla in our times, people of every religion, few know about Ashoka or Feroz Shah, but some stay for a while; and when asked why they are there, they reply that they are seeking the *barkat* / blessings—of those now dead but believed to inhabit the place as invisible spirits, the *jinns*.

Another more significant Ashokan pillar that has received much attention has now become almost a palimpsest of Indian history. This pillar is unique as its many inscriptions are indicators of extensive and direct historical statements. Currently in a central position in the Agra fort, relocated there by a Mughal ruler, it has inscribed on it a large body of Ashokan edicts in Prakrit, impressively engraved in clear-cut Brahmi letters.

Also on the pillar is the famous *prashasti* / eulogy of the Gupta ruler Samudragupta mentioning his widespread conquests and achievements. This latter inscription cuts into the first few lines of the inscription of Ashoka, suggesting that the earlier inscription could no longer be read. Or was it a deliberate attempt of the Guptas to marginalize the contents of the earlier inscription? This is unlikely, as the Gupta ruler could as well have erected a new pillar of his own. That the Gupta inscription is a *prashasti* of a Gupta ruler makes the purpose of the inscription quite clear, as it recounts why his claim to glory is justified by his great deeds. It is significant that this pillar was regarded as an appropriate object on which to engrave the eulogy. Since the earlier inscription could probably no longer be read, it was a purely symbolic understanding of the object. The sentiments expressed in the *prashasti* of Samudragupta differ, of course, from what Ashoka proclaims in his edicts on the ethical norms of governance and his negation of conquest through violence.

A few brief lines of Feroz Shah Tughlaq come next amidst some graffiti. So clearly, he was marking his attendance among the group of eminent Indian rulers. Higher up among the inscriptions is a prominent genealogy of the Mughal rulers, issued by Jahangir, and engraved in a beautiful Nastaliq script. There is a sufficient distance in space between this inscription and the earlier one. That the inscription provides the official history of the descent of the family, in effect the royal genealogy of the dynasty, is a clear indicator of its intention. It is a claim to recording the legitimacy of the dynasty and its right to rule. By integrating it into an earlier historical record, it was stating his significant contribution as a royal participant in what we would call the history of India. Jahangir had the pillar capital redecorated without altering it, and was therefore obviously proud of his association with it.

The pillar is a remarkable object encapsulating the Indian past. It was used by three major emperors over three millennia and was inscribed in three languages and scripts—the object of pride in a continuity of great Indian cultures: the Mauryan, Gupta and Mughal. For the Gupta and the Mughal, it was an act of identifying with the Indian past, the symbol of which had been created by the Maurya. The placing of this particular pillar with its antecedent inscriptions in the Agra Fort is an indirect pointer to the metaphor of a link. This seems to be supported by the minor inscriptions on these pillars perhaps conveying the same message.

Significantly, the sultans and the Mughals did not uproot these pillars and replace them with their own, nor did they destroy them, not even those that had fallen. They relocated them to places regarded as special, such as forts, citadels, mosques and suchlike, and treated them with respect. The original locations were not accidental and had been carefully planned to make a point with the public to whom Ashoka had addressed his edicts. The Gupta-period relocation of one pillar was also not incidental and carried a message involving the past. It would seem that the sultans and Mughals thought carefully about the place for the relocation of the pillars, since this too was a communication with the public. Were they also intrigued by the pillars as symbols of authority from the pre-Islamic period? Did they possibly draw elements of their own legitimacy from this object as did the Samudragupta *prashasti* many centuries before them? Were they attempting to link their history with pre-Sultanate times, thus giving a historical continuity to their dynasty? The unbroken continuity from the Tomars to the Chahamanas to the Shakas becomes formulaic when referring to the past in the popular inscriptions of the time. One wonders about what might have been the comments of the orthodoxy of both religions—Hindu and Muslim—concerning these activities. The orthodoxy is likely to have disapproved, given that none could read what was originally written on the pillars. They would have neither approved of the pillars nor respected the sentiments involved in relocating and honouring them.

16

The complexities of politics were not the only links between the Muslim rulers and the ruled. Marriage alliances were used as they often are: to explore connections or to strengthen social bonding. They eased political relations and those involved acquired allies. Members of the ruling royal families married into Rajput families of high status. Some kinship relations could be quite close despite political confrontations and differences in religion. As feudatories, some Rajputs were proximate and friendly, others could be belligerent.

Muslims were viewed as not of any *varna* / caste, and since some were in any case initially alien, they fell into the category of *mleccha* as ranked by upper-caste Hindus. Did these Rajput ruling families lose face for marrying into a *mleccha* family even if it was, at times, the imperial family? Apparently not. The marriage links were voluntary and they seem to have been happy to continue them. Was it, on the contrary, a matter of pride for them that they were marrying 'up', at least on the political scale, as it were? There was of course no love jihad in those days! Memoirs and autobiographies of various members of these families do not suggest that these marriages, even if arranged, were forced. Sociability among them on both sides was applauded. Court paintings of the imperial ateliers and book illustrations show many facets of the culture brought by the Hindu wives—particularly when celebrating festivals— which appear to have been assimilated and enjoyed by the court.

Muslim royalty and aristocracy socialized with Hindus, yet upper-caste Hindus were expected to look upon the non-Hindus such as Muslims, both aristocrats and commoners, as *mleccha*. An inscription issued by a wealthy Hindu merchant of Delhi in the fourteenth century described the current ruler, Sahavadina, that is, Shahabuddin or Muhammad bin Tughlaq, as a Turushka, and also as an almost ideal ruler. But he is also referred to as a *mleccha*. No trader would have dared to use this term for a sultan in any derogatory sense as that would have been the end of the trader. The term could only imply that the sultan had no caste identity, as was often what it meant. Yet we know that caste identities were adopted among Muslims with established ranking but perhaps not as sharply as among Hindus.

Those of low-caste and no firm caste identity would come into the category of *avarnas*. Those among them regarded as untouchable and polluting were also *mleccha*. The fourteenth-century text *Sarva-darshana-samgraha* states categorically that the *shramanas*, that is Buddhists, Jainas and Charvakas, now also included the Turushkas, since they were all technically *nastikas*—non-believers in deity. The Turushkas / Turkish Muslims did believe in a deity—Allah—but he was not a Hindu deity. On conversion, some would have carried over their caste identities, whereas others might have tried to drop them. The latter would have also been called *mleccha*. But the tenacity of caste showed its presence in non-Hindu communities as well.

17

Inevitably, migrations, invasions, the continuity of contacts introduce a range of commercial activities. These vary within themselves, from the looping trade of coastal connections or the more adventurous variety that crossed the seas, to the overland contacts over short distances, many of which grew into more complex and continuing trading exchanges. This is what happened in the second millennium AD. There was intensive trade from the Afro-Arabian coast to the Indian coast across the Arabian Sea, which brought in traders and migrants who settled in coastal India, giving rise to new communities. It also saw the arrival of overland migrants and traders from Central Asia who crossed the northern mountains into India to establish a lucrative trade, one that was extended to include Iran on the western side and northern China on the other. The Yavana / Arab and West Asian experience and the Turushka / Turkish and Central Asian experience were not the same. The Islam brought by these two categories had its differences and resulted in the evolution of diverse communities and sects, each nurturing its own diversity. This diversity has to be recognized, just as its contribution to the cultures that resulted, a subject that is now attracting the attention of historians.

Traders from Arabia and East Africa trading with the west coast of India go back many centuries, even before the birth of Islam. Extensive trade from early times touched points along the Indian Ocean arc—the coastline that can be followed from East Africa up to southern Arabia, onto the coast of Gujarat and then southwards along western coastal India to Kerala. There was considerable familiarity among traders on both sides of the Arabian Sea. After the spread of Islam, Arab traders settled in the flourishing towns along this coast. Their invading activities in the Indian subcontinent were limited to a small part of Sind, since they came more effectively as traders. The larger and more lasting activity was commercial. It lay in exporting large quantities of pepper and other spices from India, together with some textiles, and, in pre-Islamic times, importing high-value coinage along with some wine, while in later centuries, horses from Arabia.

Some Arab settlers married locally. This is what settlers often do when they arrive in new places. Cultures intermingled. All along the west coast of India, new societies evolved. Social identities and religious sects were a mix of Islam with existing religions of the area. This resulted in new religious groups, many of which are still prominent—the Khojas, Bohras, Navayaths, Mappilas and suchlike.

It also led to the employment of Arabs in local administration. These Arab officers carried out their functions under the orders of their employers, who were the Hindu rulers of the area. For example, the Rashtrakuta kings of the ninth century AD appointed a Tajik / Arab governor of the region of Sanjan on the west coast. A Rashtrakuta inscription records the grant of land made to a *brahmana* by a Tajik / Arab officer on behalf of the Rashtrakuta king. The revenue from this went towards donations to local temples as well as to the Anjuman. This could have been an Islamic organization but was more likely what the Parsis also called an Anjuman, since many Parsi merchants who had migrated from Iran were settled in Gujarat and the west coast.

Employing Arabs as high-status officials would facilitate matters relating to western trade. Even after the Arabs were settled as traders, the jobs associated with this activity such as that of officers at higher levels of administration were members of the local elite and therefore largely Hindu, and many continued in the administration of the sultans in various capacities. Arabs would also have found employment but this did not require the dismissal of earlier incumbents.

The other even more active commercial link in the first millennium AD was trade between North India and Central Asia. The trade of the Shakas and Kushans with North India at the turn of the Christian era increased in volume in the second millennium with the entry of the Turushkas. Communication between the two areas became more frequent with larger numbers participating. This in part accounts for the buildings constructed in North India at this time that were inspired by prototypes in Central Asia. Tombs and mosques imitated, to some extent, the buildings of Central Asia, but the structures used more widely in social and economic activities such as caravanserais show a more mixed aesthetic. These are indicators of an interface of cultures. The merchants in the Delhi region are said to have been wealthy. One explanation for their wealth is said to have come from the high-interest loans they advanced to the dignitaries that worked for Sultan Balban.

18

Merchants and traders were not necessarily from the same social group as the aristocrats and administrators. There is a rather unusual document from the early seventeenth century that provides us with a perspective on the life and thoughts of a merchant and his community of that time. This is the *Ardhakathanaka*, a lengthy autobiographical poem written in Braj Bhasha Hindi by Banarasidas in the time of Akbar. The author's grandfather was a *diwan* and therefore held a high ministerial position. He came from a family of jewellers but they were not extravagantly wealthy. He was schooled in a *pathshala,* the local school and then tutored by a pandit. This suggests a Brahmanical education, even if he was well versed in Jaina philosophy and religious ideas. His composition presents a view of Mughal times from the perspective of the Jaina merchant community living in Agra and Banaras, with extensive trading networks in other towns. Merchant groups were kept well occupied. Jaipur alone had many highly active markets. Banarasidas established his own shop in Agra, among many local jewellers. That this was possible, he writes, was largely because of the peace and stability of Mughal rule. This statement could be mildly exaggerated but seems unlikely to be entirely untrue.

Problems with certain Mughal officers who tried to extort money from the rich merchants are mentioned in passing with a brief comment on how they were handled. The description has a touch of the familiar! Such demands seem to have made no difference to the wealth of the merchants, which remained undiminished. This in some ways is not surprising, given that the sixteenth and seventeenth centuries was the high point of the Indian medieval economy, as is suggested by various accounts of the time and in the work of modern economic historians. Landowners in the time of Akbar are listed as being of both communities. The wealth of India was not to be sneezed at, even if the peasants living in the rural areas were poor. The wealth also came from trade and commerce rather than only the revenue from the rural economy. Hindu merchants were essential players in urban trade.

The *Ardhakathanaka* has detailed descriptions of religious practices such as the deities that were worshipped, the rituals, and the places of pilgrimage. One misses more details on the popular religions of the time, especially the Bhakti sects and the Sufis, and what their impact was. A controversial but popular Jaina movement was started in Banaras in the lifetime of Banarasidas on which he comments. Victimization is not mentioned in these reflections. It would seem that the Jainas were reasonably confident of the stability of their religion and were asserting a distinctive identity. This may well have been so. If they were being referred to as *nastika* and *mleccha* in Sanskrit texts, then having to explain their beliefs would have added to their confidence.

The merchants were not the only ones involved in commerce. Curiously, religious institutions have always been active in trade and many have acquired much wealth as a result. Hindu temples, for instance, or Sufi *khanqahs* built with royal patronage or the donations of the wealthy had to maintain themselves and keep up an impressive standard. Running an institution, such as an extensive place of worship, required not only the initial outlay of wealth but, equally importantly, a constant availability of resources for upkeep and routine mainte- nance. This meant acquiring property, therefore dona- tions of land were welcome. These are referred to in the Mughal documents.

The investment of wealth would have meant partic- ipation in commercial activities. Temples were not kept out of these activities, which were multiple. Temples were landowners, bankers, and investors in commerce. The Somanatha Temple in Gujarat controlled diverse interests that made it one of the wealthiest temples in the area. This temple has its own curious story as no two Persian sources are in agreement as to what happened when Mahmud of Ghazni raided the temple in the eleventh century AD. Every text has a different fantasy about the happenings at the raid so one wonders what actually did happen. The Sanskrit sources, by contrast, are silent or make a passing mention suggesting that the event made no deep impression on them. The silence is unlikely to be deliberate as it is so consistent in those few texts that refer to Somanatha. When, in the twelfth century, the Chaulukya king Kumarapala decided to rebuild what is said to be a dilapidated temple, a major Sanskrit text describing the events, the *Prabandhachintamani* of Merutunga, states that the dilapidation was due to the lack of maintenance by the officers concerned, and because it had weathered badly by sea spray since it was built on the seashore. No mention is made of Mahmud's raid. On being rebuilt, the temple very successfully picked up its commercial activities.

It is not surprising, therefore, to find that the Somanatha and associated temples in Saurashtra had trading interests. The Persian merchant Nuruddin Feroz, or Noradina Piroja as he is called in non-Persian sources, trading with the commercial centres of India's west coast, needed to settle some of his people who had come with him as traders and employees in Saurashtra. He requested a donation of some land for building a mosque. The land was donated to him by the local civic body that included those controlling the assets of the temples, a part of which was included in the donation. The negotiations involved the chief priest, Tripurantaka.

19

Inscriptions carry a variety of information depending on who is issuing them. Thus, some social activities and donations of merchants find mention. Since I have just mentioned the *Ardhakathanaka*, a trader's autobiography, let me turn to some inscriptions from the community of merchants that complement the text as a source. A clutch of inscriptions was issued by Hindu merchants living in the vicinity of Delhi during the Sultanate rule around the fourteenth to sixteenth centuries. Some record the donation of wells in the area. In a few instances, the ancestors of the donors are said to have come from Ucch and Multan, both being locations focused on the trade across the mountains with Afghanistan, Iran and Central Asia. Horses coming from these areas were much valued as was the export of spices, textiles and, later, indigo.

The genealogies of the families mentioned in the inscriptions are given in some detail, both men and women having Hindu names. This was perhaps to establish their own status and historical antecedents. The currently ruling sultan is named and his origin is frequently given as Shaka or Turushka. The current Shaka ruler was often preceded by the Rajput dynasties of Tomaras and Chahamanas. The continuity of the names is striking and there was no disjuncture between the Chahamanas and the Shakas. The ruling sultan is praised for his benevolent rule. If this is exaggeration, it is impressive that the same sentiment, even if formulaic, is repeated elsewhere too.

Whether it was purely formulaic or a common convention, there isn't a mention of malevolent rulers. This, of course, is familiar from the formulaic style of the earlier *prashastis* of Hindu kings with their sustained, if not exaggerated, praise for the ruler. The stylistic echoes are recognizable. The contents, of course, differ. The language is Sanskrit barring a small number that has a mix of Sanskrit and Persian, presumably reflecting the speech of elite groups of that time. The opening invocation is to Hindu deities such as Shiva and Ganesha, embedded in fulsome flattery. The lengthier compositions are authored by named *brahmana* pandits.

Other inscriptions from further afield record a number of economic transactions that seem to have continued undisturbed at least among the Hindu elite of the time. The names of creditors or bankers and debtors are mentioned, and sometimes the money involved. In one inscription, mention is made of the gifting of fertile, cultivable land involving the maharajas Dharam Singh and Jai Singh, some *brahmanas* and a few others. This was probably a record of a grant of land in accordance with earlier practice. Even in earlier times there was occasionally a nexus between wealthy landowners and merchants, with investments from the former in commercial enterprises, although the major activity remained in the hands of merchants. The *thakkura* owning land could mutate into the *vanik* or trader, or at least finance the *vanik* to some degree. This faintly echoes the practice in the initial urban centres of the Ganges plain when a few *gahapati*s / heads of household, who were often landowners, took to commerce and became *setthi*s / merchants. *Setthi-gahapati* is a category known to the Buddhist texts.

This was probably the group that felt the maximum pressure of having to pay the *jaziya* / tax on non-Muslims, which was imposed by some of the rulers. Not surprisingly, this tax was under debate as to whether it should or should not be levied by the government. Akbar was opposed to it, in part perhaps because it created an unnecessary differentiation among his subjects, whereas Aurangzeb was in favour of levying it. Taxes of course are never entirely arbitrary or whimsical. The nudging of a fiscal crisis, however marginal, would encourage the thought of further taxes. Even a small tax helps. It is worth thinking about if the economy of the empire was healthier in the sixteenth century than it was in the eighteenth. A fiscal crisis is a disaster and is feared, and this can lead to extreme actions by those in authority. We know this from the eleventh-century example of Harshadeva, the king of Kashmir, who, despite being

Hindu, took to looting temples in order to obtain the required wealth to keep himself and the kingdom afloat.

However, the Turushkas are not always regarded with admiration as they are in the inscriptions of the merchants. There are situations in which hostile remarks are made and the context of these have relevance. There are inscriptions in Sanskrit issued by Hindu rulers defeated in battle against the Turushkas. They refer to their own Hindu ancestors—projected as heroes—who are said to have ousted the Turushkas in earlier times. Now the defeated Hindu kings refer angrily to the Turushka victors as their *mleccha* enemies, using the term in a derogatory sense, who don't hesitate to kill cows and *brahmanas*. The projection is far from complimentary as would be expected from the defeated. This is an incident when there is malevolence attributed to the victor by the defeated.

20

Let me turn to those at the lower level of social ranking in those times. Groups with specialized employment potential, such as weavers, carpenters or masons and suchlike, seem to have been comfortable in their work despite their caste. An inscription of 1199 AD found on a stone fragment in the Qutab Minar is composed in Hindi and written in the Nagari script. It is a benediction asking for good fortune to be bestowed on Malikdin. The location of the inscription is described as being on a *kirti-stambha*, which was well known as a category of hero-stones on which the act of a person who has performed a celebratory action is recorded.

More precise inscriptions are available in the fourteenth century, after the Qutab Minar in Delhi was struck by lightning and required repairs. The masons who carried out the repairs left a scatter of inscriptions all over recording the repairs. These inscriptions were embedded at various points in and around the Minar. The language is local Hindi, engraved in the Nagari script. These are short records of those who worked at the site and express their gratitude to the deity whom they worshipped and who was said to have ensured the success of their work.

Significantly, the dates are in the Samvat era and not the Hijri era. The name of the sultan, given in its Hindi form, which is probably what was generally used, and under whose patronage the repairs were carried out, is mentioned, but just that. Hindu deities are invoked. The dynastic succession goes predictably from Tomar and Chauhan Rajputs to the Shakas—as the current rulers are described. These inscriptions were composed largely by *brahmana* pandits, a few being mentioned by name. Those responsible for doing the repairs are named and they were Hindus. There was an architect— Chahada the son of Devapala. The masons are also named—Lashman, Nana, Solha, Lola, Harimani Gaveri the son of Sahadhaira, and suchlike. The inscriptions conclude by invoking the deity they worship, often Ganesha and Shiva, and more frequently the particular deity worshipped by craftsmen, Vishvakarma, by whose grace, they state, the job was completed successfully.

Invoking their deity clarifies that it was not forced labour, nor the labour of converts. Fourteenth-century inscriptions refer to the carpenter Dharmavanini and the engraver Vishnukantha. Such inscriptions are not unique to the Qutab Minar as they are also found in other buildings elsewhere. A fourteenth-century inscription also on a pillar in the cloister of a mosque refers to Kamau the son of the *shilpi* Visadru as the architect probably working in the Lal Darwaza Masjid in Jaunpur. Their employment in these technical jobs continues.

These inscriptions are of those employed by the administration, dated in the Samvat era, composed in Sanskrit—sometimes faulty, written in the Nagari script—and they evoke Hindu deities. The participants in the activity recorded in the inscriptions refer to the completion of a job in a normal matter-of-fact way without any obstruction. The architects, masons, craftsmen, carpenters and engravers mentioned in the inscriptions were Hindus. They were obviously employed freely, judging by the inscriptions that they engraved, and which they located within the buildings constructed by those who employed them. Stylistically and linguistically, they continued the norms of pre-Islamic days even if the subject matter differed.

To describe Hindus at this time as enslaved is problematic, to put it mildly, as the information from various sources does not suggest this. For instance, in the seventeenth century, the emperor Shah Jahan had a monopoly on the indigo trade extending throughout the Mughal Empire. It is said that the monopoly was given to a Hindu merchant which affected the price of indigo and this in turn impoverished the peasants who grew it. So they objected to the changed monopoly and it was finally revoked. Mention is also made of zamindars or landowners, such as Churaman, Gokul and others, mobilizing Jat peasants and encouraging revolts. An official of Aurangzeb's government, Ishardas Nagar, mentions that the peasantry observed a mixture of religions and their religious identity could not be easily ascertained. This

would also have applied to low-caste others. That peasants could be mobilized to revolt, whatever the reasons
might be, does not sound like the activity of an enslaved
population.

21

One of the problems with focusing largely on one category of sources is that the emergent picture is not fully representative. We also have to state what the others thought. Because of the insistence on referring to the second millennium AD as the 'Muslim' period, the Persian chronicles were given greater attention than other sources. The history of Somanatha illustrates this point. The greater dependence on one set of sources—the Persian texts—led to ignoring sources in other languages. Thus, the focus was on only one aspect of the history. But if one turns to sources in Sanskrit, such as inscriptions, texts of the Jainas and others, then the earlier picture changes to the point where alternative explanations for the events in Somanatha have also to be debated.

From the perspective of historiography, the agenda of colonial writers is distinctly different from others. As has been said earlier, British historians who mention Somanatha reiterate the colonial view as given by Edward Gibbon, James Mill and others, and in the Henry Eliot and John Dowson collection, in their references to Indian history. This view continued unchallenged and was in part responsible for state policy as well. When in 1842, Ellenborough ordered the British general fighting in Afghanistan to bring back what were said to be the gates from the Somanatha Temple, looted by Mahmud of Ghazni, he took pride in claiming that by this act he had avenged the insult of eight hundred years on the Hindus. Was this the cue to Hindu religious nationalists who made a similar statement when breaking down the Babri Masjid in 1992? The gates, as it turned out, were not from the Somanatha temple but more likely from a monument in Egypt!

The constant reference to invasions and destruction blacked out the more significant historical change in India during these centuries. Invasions are both devastating in terms of violence and destructive of cultures. But the aftermath can be, and often is, the evolution of new socio-economic interests and new cultures. This does not justify invasions but suggests a less negative outcome. In inverted ways, invasions open up contacts if those who invade settle in the conquered land in which they invest their wealth and labour. This can take the form of continuity in occupations such as the ones I have mentioned earlier—trade, architecture and masonry—together with the adjustments that they introduce. Where the conqueror is curious about and respects the intellectual activities of the conquered ones, as clearly both the Yavanas and the Turushkas did, there the result can be a remarkable intellectual exchange, sometimes with unexpected results extending from philosophy to architecture.

One manifestation of this in medieval India was the dialogue between Hindu and Muslim scholars and teachers, both fluent in Sanskrit and Persian, which resulted in much literary interchange. This was at a different level from the experiences already referred to, as it had to do with the intellectual life of cultures, some of which maintained a distinctive difference while others coalesced into shortening if not negating the distance. Such experiences are a constant in the histories of every society, but are more frequent in societies such as those of the Indian subcontinent, where the arrival of new settlers gave rise to new cultures.

Poets, philosophers and scholars from Central Asia and Persia arrived at the Indian courts where many settled and established their centres, resulting in the evolution of new cultural formulations. There was a spurt of intellectual activities, more so in Mughal times. Some were enlivened by the cross-currents of thought and possible fresh articulations. Others, more orthodox, disapproved of this interface of cultures and what were seen as activities that were contrary to the norms of religious observance. The Sanskrit-knowing literati at these courts, knowledgeable in Persian as well, helped translate Sanskrit texts into Persian. Among the latter were the *Yoga Vasishtha* and the *Bhagavad Gita* which were essential to understanding Hindu belief. Persian scholars learnt Sanskrit in order to work on translations.

The translation of fundamental texts such as the *Mahabharata* and the *Ramayana* or literary anthologies such as the *Kathasaritasagara* was heavy-going but was nevertheless insisted upon by imperial patrons. Biographies of kings had earlier been present in the Sanskrit *charita* literature and in similar Persian texts, as also anthologies of poems and the all-important dictionaries. Ensuring proficiency in both languages helped bring literary interests on par. Upper-caste scholars of Sanskrit also wrote in Persian. Included among them was a prominent *brahmana* member of Aurangzeb's court, Chandar Bhan, a person of considerable standing in the Indo-Persian world of literature apart from his status in the Mughal system. Much of the literature was now also being composed in emergent regional languages and was therefore accessible to a far larger audience.

Religious literature in Sanskrit and Hindi was of particular interest to various Sufi sects, some interested in the ideas of the Bhakti teachers and some who had expertise in varieties of Yoga and the earlier philosophical schools. The range of religious ideas among these various sects in India triggered off a further exploration, outside the boundaries of the orthodox. This brought about an expansive range of teaching and discussion that needs to be studied from a comparative perspective. The long-standing debates in the Punjab between the Sufis and the Nath yogis are being currently read with much interest by scholars. Nor should we forget that it was Dara Shukoh, the sibling of Aurangzeb, who projected the *Upanishads* as significant religious literature. His was not a lone voice.

The intellectual background of this cultural interaction remains incomplete without mention of the crucial role of various subjects that might perhaps be described as proto-sciences: mathematics, astronomy and medicine. These were subjects being worked on and developed in various locations in India and were also flourishing in places elsewhere such as Baghdad and Samarkand. Considerable use was made of this knowledge even in India as is demonstrated by the observatories for astronomy that were built by Raja Jai Singh of Amber, a feudatory of the Mughals. All this would have involved much translating, given that the texts were in Sanskrit, Persian, Arabic and Chinese. The knowledge they contain is regarded as advanced, as for example in arithmetic and algebra—in the *Lilavati* and the *Bijaganita*—or in the working out of calculus. The question, therefore, that has been raised on occasion is why this knowledge was not developed further in the cultures of these languages. Were there parallel advances in other areas of knowledge? By this time Europe itself had made contact with Asia.

22

Let me conclude by asking the obvious question. Given all this activity of Hindus at every social level and across time in the second millennium AD, what does this tell us about inter-community relations during that time? Shouldn't the educated Indians of today, as inheritors of this history, assess the relations through greater knowledge of its activity and understand it? As with fake news, fake anything creates immense problems regarding what to accept and what to discard. For us historians, studying the past means understanding how the past came to be—through a logical and rational explanation. If we are to understand the roots of our culture, we have to give deep attention to comprehending the extensive inter-community relations of the past—both the harmonious and the conflictual. We have to provide explanations, based on reliable evidence, as to what happened and why. Superficial generalizations are as good as useless.

The evidence for inter-community relations points to a situation similar to that of what had existed earlier: they could be accommodative and harmonious in some situations or could be aggressive in others. Each category of relationship has to be carefully examined and the cause determined. To describe the entire range of relations as invariably the victimization of the Hindus by the Muslims is not borne out by the evidence. Such sweeping generalizations carry no weight among historians.

The next step is to ask why certain controversies have arisen in present times, which although pertaining to the here and now nevertheless seek endorsement from the past. How do we analyse and assess what is claimed as having happened in the past if there is no proven evidence to support the claim? It is crucial to separate that which can be proved from that which is fantasy or hearsay.

In discussing inter-community relations between Hindus and Muslims in the second millennium AD, my intention is not to deny that there were conflicts. In every period of Indian history, there have been conflicts over religious ideas or socioeconomic forms presented in a religious garb. As I have already mentioned, in earlier times it was some sects of Shaivas in conflict with some of the Buddhists and Jainas, and then there were sects of Shaivas and Vaishnavas in conflict, or there were Hindu kings looting Hindu temples. Conflicts can either have a marginal effect or can be devastating, depending on how serious they are. The severity of the suppression of the untouchables was far greater than the conflicts between *brahmanas* and *shramanas*. Whatever the period of history, wherever there is evidence of conflict, that evidence has to be analysed and explained. It should not be set aside in an effort to project an altogether harmonious past in some period and the reverse in others. We still have to explain why Buddhism was reduced to a whisper in many places in India where previously it had had a strong presence. The Turushkas and suchlike added Islam to the religions involved in these relationships. It is equally important to recognize that in inter-community relationships of whatever kind, religion is not the sole determining factor. Many kinds of relationships are present in which religion plays only a marginal role, if at all.

Religions run into trouble when they become political weapons, as some religious sects became—and some are becoming. Aurangzeb's donations to *brahmanas* and temples were more likely motivated by politics as they were not acts of religion. Royal patronage may be homage to a religious belief or even a healthy donation to keep a place of worship going, be it a temple, a monastery or a mosque. There is always the fear of a large-scale institution going into decline through neglect should the donation not be forthcoming. Religious buildings becoming derelict are frequently the result of a shortage of funds for maintenance. Safeguarding property can sometimes lead to a further nexus between the religious institution and political authority. Where a religious building is constructed substantially by a political authority such as a king, there it becomes the symbol of political power. Where there is a competition for patronage, there the potentially political factor comes into play.

Historical analysis is therefore concerned with investigating whether a conflict is in fact due to religious factors *per se*; whether every conflict involving persons of diverse religions can be automatically labelled a religious conflict. There can be many causes of conflict and these causes have to be identified in terms of what was central and what was peripheral, if at all. Society does not move permanently on a single axis. To generalize and state that all relationships between groups belonging to different religions—Hindu and Muslim, for instance—would invariably have been only of one kind, namely, dictated by religion, and would invariably have had only one predictable consequence, namely conflict, is not history but a surrender to an explanation no longer viable. The historian would have to examine the evidence carefully, assess the possibilities comparatively, and then put forth an explanation.

My plea is that the history taught to our children and grandchildren in schools should be based on reliable evidence and should preferably be the more thoughtful history of professional historians. Each generation inherits history and uses it as the base to build its own identity and culture. If the base is faulty and has empty spaces in its telling where historical evidence has been disfigured, or arbitrarily altogether removed, then in such situations it can be said that the history has been distorted—as has happened recently in the removal of significant data from history textbooks published by the NCERT. This is unacceptable to historians and should be unacceptable to those being taught history. The arbitrary removal of a large body of knowledge and segments of other information in any discipline distorts the discipline and its validity. It can only lead to the destruction of that knowledge as an entity.

It is an insult to professional historians when institutions under government control arbitrarily discard historical data from what is taught as history. A history with deliberately gouged-out portions can only be erroneous. It comes from a mindset that is not only anti-intellectual but also has little respect for the disciplines that go into the making of an educational system. A discipline has to be complete since it is always open to discussion. For some decades now, a few of us have been arguing that textbooks and theoretical books used in teaching history should be entirely in the hands of professionals, such as trained historians assisted by trained teachers. The same applies to all other subjects as well—sciences, social sciences and humanities. Those that are not trained in the methodology of a discipline cannot do justice to that discipline.

By suggesting a more in-depth examination of inter-community relations, I am not arguing that relations between communities over the last three thousand years, or even earlier, have always been amicable. And this is not confined to India. Inter-community relations in every society or civilization, kingdom or empire have had problematic moments, irrespective of whether this pertains to the past or to now. Groups that live amicably may possibly change as they evolve and on occasion this may introduce conflict. It is necessary to distinguish between what actually was a source of conflict in the past and what we today want to project as the source of conflict because it suits current political requirements. The conflicts of the past, depending on their causes, were either resolved or else social adjustments were made that permitted the continuation of social functioning. Or, sometimes, the conflict continued but took other shapes and forms.

In early times too, there were problems, as I have pointed out, but we have glossed over them and given them little attention. This was because we wanted to maintain that all was harmonious in India in pre-Islamic times. We avoid discussing the problems of those early times and observing how both consensus and dissent in those times contributed to shaping our culture. If the past is subjected to critical inquiry, we may succeed in exploring the causes of conflict and the termination or mutation of such causes—an exercise that may help us in settling problems of present times as well. For instance, the communal problem of today is nurtured on a so-called 'history' that is historically untenable.

Perhaps we should remind ourselves of some of the problems from the past. Why does the most powerful of all Indian emperors, Ashoka Maurya, call for harmonious relations between the various religious sects—such as the *brahmanas*, *shramanas* and others—if there wasn't some disharmony among them? The same appeal is heard later from time to time and more so when there are historical changes of some magnitude. In assessing these situations and what causes them, we have to be careful not to stray from the evidence and give vent to our imagination in constructing the past—whether as pleasant or unpleasant.

Among the examples of this world of fantasies, currently being floated in various kinds of media and in some public speeches, and on many other platforms, is the question that I have drawn attention to as being more pertinent to contemporary politics than to the inter-community history of India in medieval times. The question is whether there really was a victimization of the Hindus by the Muslims or is this a convenient red rag to the bull? Are its manifestations now replacing an intelligent understanding of the politics of inter-community relations expressed in religious and other forms in medieval times in India? Instead of gathering reliable evidence and asking thoughtful questions of the evidence that will help explain the actual relations between communities, or at least come close to that, there is an attempt to construct a fantasized history, lacking in evidence, merely to justify the present-day assertion of power by one community over others. This latter attitude appeals to the ambitions of some contemporaries but it neither represents nor attempts to understand the history of earlier times.

The make-believe history that arises out of the stirrings of religious nationalism, and is necessary to the legitimation of such nationalism, will not leave us until the political need for religious nationalism to be controlling public thought no longer exists. The confrontation between the trained, professional historians and those quite untrained but claiming to know history will continue until such time as the history constructed by the latter ceases to be a political weapon. This process can be accelerated if trained historians become more assertive and object to their discipline being mauled.

The media today is crucial to the construction of social and political attitudes. The issues, whether fake or authentic, are central to both citizens and the state. Where the state has a grip on the media, it thereby also has an overwhelming role in propagating ideologies for general consumption. Citizens are at the receiving end of these projections. Prior to accepting or rejecting these, citizens should assert their right of either allowing this willingly or questioning and debating the message that is being imprinted on their thinking.

This is a concern of much substance because the media in the last few years has, in many parts of the world, become an institution that can play a substantial role in either strengthening democracy or breaking it— no less so in India. If it is to speak truth to power, as it claims to be doing, then it cannot afford to sell fake news or support fake information. What it projects has to be based on proven, reliable evidence. This is not impossible, given the variation in existing media platforms where even if many are currently thought to be unreliable, there might be some rare ones that remain concerned about the reliability of the statements they put out.

In the present day, the media has become the social institution that seeks, through the information it provides, to educate the public. Therefore, as with all else in society, the media must also meet ethical norms. These may currently have faded but are hopefully not dead and can be resuscitated. We cannot allow ethics to be leached out of our social functioning. We can at least demand proven evidence for explanations that we are given for many aspects of both the present and the past. Areas of thought such as history that have a powerful role in the politics of the present would be rendered useless if allowed to be distorted in order to service political bastions. Areas of thought have to be protected by the freedom to debate and discuss issues of contention. In short, there has to be the freedom of self-expression in forms that are nonviolent. Both these are being systematically curtailed with little effective comment from the media.

As in all inter-community relations, interactions can and do change over time. They can be so cordial that diverse cultures get quietly knit together and emerge as a single entity. Yet at other times there can be conflict between them that can be disruptive. This applies to the past as much as to the present. The same explanation is not valid century after century. We may think that our society in the past was static but all societies undergo change frequently, as the study of history teaches us. Every substantial change is linked to historical change and the historian has to explain the change. Explanations, as we all know, do alter when there is fresh reliable evidence or when new questions are asked. This is precisely what every generation of historians is now doing—searching for fresh sources of information and asking new questions, and probing further the information that we already have. The aftermath of the change is what is commented upon, especially when assessing the impact on society of subsequent actions. The weariness about what is happening today in the history supported by authority comes from the fact that we are being drawn through the same arguments that were discussed a century ago and have been discarded by professional historians.

For the study of the second millennium AD, the major sources have been Persian chronicles, court literature of the Sultanates and the Mughals, and the accounts of various persons from Europe and other places visiting India in the capacity of traders, missionaries and diplomats. Added to this is the writing of the Sanskrit-knowing upper castes commenting on their own times. These perspectives are largely those of how various elites of that time saw the Indian world.

There are also many perspectives that are manifest in other kinds of sources and more so in the literature of the regional languages. These sources cannot be juxtaposed and left at that. The two have to be integrated to obtain a perspective of the complete social landscape. Their interface has to be studied. Are the Sanskrit royal biographies or fragmented pieces of history of the many feudatories of the Mughal empire, continuing the pre-Islamic *charita* and *vamshavali* traditions of historical biographies and chronicles, or, influenced by Persian chronicles and texts, and to what extent? Given that there was an intellectual exchange of thought through the languages used, the mutual influence of forms would be expected.

This relates to the question of why we research and study history. It begins with a curiosity about ourselves. Who are we, what are our origins and what have we made of ourselves? Understanding the past brings clarity to understanding the present—but it has to be as close as possible to the actual past. This requires dependence on reliable evidence and a meticulous exploration of the possible sources that can be used. It cannot be based on a make-believe past that can be reformulated as and how we want it to be. This is the profound difference between the professional historian constantly asking questions of the data in order to clarify the understanding of it, and drawing on critical inquiry when investigating a subject, as against the person untrained in the methods of historical analysis for whom history is just a narrative about the past, and so constructed that it can be manipulated for legitimizing a particular type of present, irrespective of whether that legitimacy has any justification or not.

Do we take the trouble to recognize that the discipline of history, initially taught to us and subsequently what we read, can help us understand our culture, the people we live with, our attitudes to religion, our rights and obligations as citizens of a nation-state, all this and much more? Do we check and inquire into why in the past there were situations of confrontations sandwiched between harmonious times? And what caused each of them? How does the impact of peace or aggression determine the creation of our culture? It makes little historical sense to describe a period as consistently harmonious with no discordant note, because even in the best of times some degree of disharmony would have been and is present. Every religion proclaims that it knows the truth about life and even the afterlife. Who can speak about the latter? Perhaps the dead do speak! History requires us to push ourselves more to ask questions and understand ourselves and the world we live in. The reality lies behind the cloud of our immediate surround.

There was once a time not s0 long ago when history was just a narrative about the past. It was put together from everybody's remembrances of past events and people, and also from whatever documents that might have existed among families and friends, and, for that matter, whatever memories could be culled from wherever there was some reference to the past. This material was slowly refined and fine-tuned to the extent that history became a narrative of the past pertinent to much of society and the evidence on which it was based could be tested for reliability. History developed what these days is called a methodology, a procedure first propounded in the sciences which became one of the essentials of critical inquiry and the process of reconstructing the past. A methodology is now foundational to the study of the social sciences—of which history is a part.

But then history began to play a bigger role in questions of identity and the past. It was no longer the identity of a person, a family or a community. It became the identity of society as a whole. This was essential to the construction of nationalism. History now had a bigger purpose than just reconstructing a simple straightforward story of the past. It had to explain what happened in the past, when and why it happened and how, so that we could better understand both the past and its aftermath. We have also to understand the social and political situations in which a perspective of history is closely linked to the present.

To return to the metaphor of Eric Hobsbawm. Should we let the relationship between the poppy and the heroin addict remain as is? Or should we insist that the heroin addict must question or even contextualize the visions seen by her or him? Or should we reassess the quality of the opium? All knowledge advances by asking questions of it. We have to question *our* history to ensure the validity of our identity, but we also have to constantly question what passes for *their* history—the history manufactured by those claiming their narratives to be history, even if they are not, and the utilization of this construction in contemporary politics. It is through such questioning that we get to know not only whose history is being written but also why it is being done.

When we check the evidence quoted—if at all it is quoted—and the generalizations drawn from it, only then will we know whether it is professionally assessed, reliable history or if it is the concoction of those indulging in political fantasies. Is it our history or is it their history? Whose history is it?

The 'Rationalizing' of Indian History by the NCERT

Soon after I had completed the first draft of this book came the announcement that the NCERT (National Council for Education Research and Training) was deleting large sections from the existing textbooks in various subjects that were being taught in government schools. This was supposedly to ease the burden on the school child subsequent to the Covid-19 pandemic. But when scholars in each discipline looked carefully at what was being deleted, it became clear that the intention was more political and ideological. In some ways this was predictable and few of us were surprised, although we were surprised at the nonchalance with which the history syllabus had been taken apart. What was left was a rather tattered, uninspiring textbook pertaining to a crucial discipline. I wrote an article for the *Wire* which I am including here as an afterword because, in some ways, there is now a deep connection between how history is being defined and being taught.

***

The recent controversy over the deletions of sections of the textbooks in Indian history written for Classes VI to XII and published by the NCERT raises a multitude of questions. Some of these have been discussed in the recent justified anger over the dismissive treatment of important historical statements and segments in the history textbooks, currently facing a hatchet job as part of our present system of education. I would like to comment on three facets of this controversy: Why are textbooks crucial to education? What is the significance of the seemingly arbitrary hacking of earlier versions of Indian history in these textbooks? What is the immediate purpose of doing so?

Textbooks serve at least three functions. One is that they bring together the basic information required to understand a discipline. Ideally, this is updated every decade. Updating does not mean deleting, whether this be just a sentence or a paragraph or an entire section or chapter. Updating means the infusion of new knowledge or arguments and readings on the basis of new knowledge. The books are graded in a hierarchy from the simple ones used in junior classes to the more complex ones used in senior classes. This cannot be treated as merely a repetition of the lower at the higher level, as it is a deliberate change in the level of comprehension and upgrading of information. There is therefore a difference in how history is treated in the books used in the two classes at two different levels.

Secondly, good textbooks teach and encourage students to ask relevant questions that enhance their knowledge of the subject they are studying. Asking questions and, preferably, probing questions in any discipline is essential to enhancing knowledge. This is ideally what education is meant to encourage. Thirdly, the textbook is an aid to the teacher in teaching a subject and explaining why that subject has significance in our society and culture. What and how children are taught is the key to the kind of citizens they will become, as is the claim of the Jesuits, the Rashtriya Swayamsevak Sangh and many other organizations.

Textbooks therefore deserve to be taken seriously and be given the kind of attention they received when the NCERT books, Sets I and II, were being written. Set I was written in the 1960s and 70s and, subsequently, Set II consisted of the ones that replaced the earlier ones in 2006. But when textbooks have been hacked, then one knows that education is not the primary purpose of this action. The actual concern is to nurture citizens that are content with what they are taught by those in authority, without in any way questioning it. It is important to reiterate that education should not be just learning the alphabet and being able to read primers. It has to encourage thinking beyond the obvious, which requires a far larger financial slice of the budget than is currently given, and there is a need to train school teachers to encourage school children to ask relevant questions in order to understand the world in which we live. In this, the teacher-training programmes need considerable improvement as also the availability of books in school libraries. The study of history plays a central role in normal pedagogy.

History is based on a continuity of events. It makes little sense to delete large sections of it, as such deletions inevitably confuse both teachers and students. Thus, to jump from the early to the late second millennium AD, and to preferably avoid teaching 'Muslim history' can only result in immense confusion. What happened in all these centuries is a question that has to be answered, followed by why this history is not being taught. Discussion of the impact of events gets stymied if there are breaks that create huge blanks in the narrative, or else deletions that annul the centrality of discussing an event in order to understand it or observing connections between various actions. Can one really discuss the assassination of a major political leader—in this case, Mahatma Gandhi—without mentioning who exactly the assassin was, what were his possible motives and what was the political aftermath of the event?

History is not a string of events with dates attached. Discussing the context of an event is crucial to its historical understanding. This is equally applicable when discussing why a particular community was targeted and killed in large numbers on a particular occasion. Such actions cannot just be blanked out by removing mention of them in textbooks, as has been done in the NCERT textbook with the Gujarat killings of 2002. These events survive as a part of social memory and are spoken of both publicly and in quietude. They become the subject of other books and debates and are not forgotten. This has been the fate of the Holocaust, the

Gulag, some would say even the Partition of India in 1947, and similar historical happenings.

Predictably the pronouncements of the changes made by the NCERT in the all-India school textbooks come within a cloud of confusion. Two aspects, among others, of what has been said are puzzling as their purpose is unclear. One is what is meant by what the NCERT calls 'rationalizing'. The other is that the justification for deleting the sentences, passages and chapters from the school textbooks, especially those for Class XI and XII, has not been explained in each case as it should have been. How does it ease the burden of post-Covid studies if the sentence referring to the assassin of Gandhi being a *brahmana* is removed?

To rationalize what has been written means that the choice of how and why a text is written is determined by rational and logical explanations of the data. The reason for what is deleted from an existing text has to be explained and from the same perspective. The choice should not be arbitrary or casual or unconcerned with the subject of the text, nor a subjective whim conforming to an obvious ideology. Rationalization means giving a logically justifiable explanation for the changes being made. The mere deletion of sentences, paragraphs, sections or chapters in a text is not in itself a rationalization, but is rather a rationing of what is being presented. Has the NCERT confused 'rationalizing' with 'rationing' and has simply axed large portions of the textbooks in order to claim that the students now have less to study?

Rationing means to cut down, to prune, to delete—which is precisely what the NCERT has done.

The more sensible way of doing this—if the weight of the Covid disturbance has to be met—would be to leave the textbook as is and simply state which sections would not be examined, although they could be read by the students. It would not, of course, have let the NCERT off the hook, but it would have made some sense at least in accommodating the syllabus to students suffering from the after effects of Covid. It would have left the history intact and of much interest to the brighter students who use Book XII as the starting point for asking questions. But this was obviously not treated in a logical and rational way, so it is clear that Covid was not the reason for making the changes. The changes appear to have been made to suit the ideology of those in control of the content of textbooks, who were determined that the history taught officially should be in conformity with this ideology. Deletions have to be justified with rational explanations pertaining to the text itself, namely, why particular sentences or sections of the text were chosen for deletion and not others. When looked at closely, there is a deliberate plan in what has been deleted—as many commentators have pointed out—and to which the NCERT has no coherent answer. No doubt the plan will be explicit when Set III of the NCERT textbooks, written by their own team of experts, will be published.

If an event that happened in the past is worthy of being referred to in a history textbook for Class XII, then what matters is not just a mention of the event but also a discussion of what happened, when it happened, how it happened and why it happened. In a period of 600 years, from AD 1200 to 1800, the Medieval Period as it is called, if the contents have to be reduced, then the solution is not to just erase three hundred years of history—a major chunk of history—but to select fewer major events from the larger span of time and discuss those, whilst decreasing the space given to the less important. In other words, the historian has to select what are thought to be the more significant historical events.

Deleting pages and chapters can only be described as an unthinking way of reducing content. Given that the NCERT has not convincingly explained the reasons behind the choice of the deletions and the viability of such actions in historical study, we can only assume that the intention was not to improve the quality of the text-book but to push a particular reading of history, as demanded by those who dictated the choice of deletions. So much for the intellectual independence of the educational system in our country.

Another confusion has been pointed out by many, but it persists. Which are the books and the historians whose histories are thus being obliterated? The NCERT textbooks in history were first written in the 1960s and 70s, and their authors were Romila Thapar, Arjun Dev, R. S. Sharma, Satish Chandra and Bipan Chandra. These were the books that the Morarji Desai government tried to ban, but the government itself fell before this could be done.

Nevertheless, the historians who wrote these books were disapproved of by the BJP in no uncertain terms. They were accused of being Marxists, leftists, academic and intellectual terrorists, and authors writing a distorted history. This was followed, as usual, by the predictable litany of abuse. It reflected a fear of rational history as against the laughable fantasies of their particular constructions of history. The BJP government in 1999 ordered new textbooks to be written by another set of historians who were willing to write the kind of history that suited the politics of the Sangh Parivar. These too could not come into circulation properly as the government was voted out in 2004.

The UPA government, led by the Congress, came to power and decided on a new set of textbooks, the first set now being forty years old. The new set, Set II as it were, was written by historians who had not earlier written textbooks for the NCERT and who introduced a new historical orientation that was approved of by professional historians and that could not all be labelled as obviously Marxist. When they were prescribed, these textbooks were attacked by some of the more articulate leftists as having conceded too much to the new kind of history writing and not being radical (in the old sense of the word) enough. The confusion in all this now is that the books of Set II are currently disapproved of by the supporters of Hindutva, but their authors are hardly mentioned. Therefore, the personal attacks which are now carried out are on historians disapproved of by the present government; they are essentially those who were the authors of the books of Set I, which, incidentally, have not been in use for two decades now. Since the authors of the Set II books are not attacked by name, it is the earlier authors that continue to face the brunt. These five authors are the more familiar names and some have been abused without pause for the last fifty years. And of those five authors, four are no more and the last one is anyway ageing!

Each time the government changed, the textbooks were also sought to be changed. The coinciding of a change in government requiring a change in textbooks happened so often that it became the butt of jokes. Some of us, therefore, wrote a strong letter to the UPA government in 2005 arguing that the writing of textbooks in all disciplines should not be under the control of any government institution but, rather, in the hands of the professionals in the discipline, preferably the more reputable professionals. A choice of experts by professionals in the discipline would certainly be more impressive than those chosen by government agencies. Disciplines are now highly specialized and require expertise and training. Textbooks cannot be left to those that are not properly trained in the discipline and its methodology. Needless to say, our letters and reminders remained unanswered. But of course, no political party was willing to concede our request, as each is only concerned with capturing the minds of the young, not teaching the young how to think and question the world around them. When citizens learn to think and question independently, those in authority have to answer their questions. This approach has now been substantially washed away. Education is becoming just a catechism. It does not teach the young to question and to think independently.

We have to concede that putting together a syllabus is a complicated and time-consuming exercise. I recall the lengthy, in-depth discussions we had with the authors on the history syllabus in the meetings of the committee that oversaw the NCERT Set 1 textbooks. Items put forward were discussed in terms of the evidence that supported them, their role in the wider history of that moment, and its aftermath. Activities were seen from multiple perspectives to determine their significance. This meant debates on many items.

In the writing of the NCERT Set 2 textbooks, the same procedure was followed when the syllabus was drawn up. The discussion by those who participated in it was very thorough. The history narrated was more up to date but the procedure was the same. Before an item of history was accepted for inclusion or declined, there was much debate. The committee involved in this consisted of more than those contributing to the book and included other experts in the subject as well. This procedure was evidently not followed by the NCERT in the recent decisions to delete sections of the textbooks. From public statements by the NCERT and its teams, there was only one main official reason for making deletions, namely, lessening the burden on school children after Covid. Cutting out repetition from Class VI to Class XII makes little sense since obviously the way events are taught in Class VI will not be the same as in Class XII—or should not be. It was not a repetition but a higher level of perception. Arguing that the deleting of sections of the text because of the burden of Covid on students does not in any way whatsoever explain why particular historical statements or selected histories were deleted. It is crucial to know this in any circumstance and more so here. Going through the list of deletions as listed in the booklets, it becomes clear that the purpose has little to do with the workload on the students. It is more clearly the intention to support a particular interpretation of history, one acceptable to those currently in power. The deletions are not arbitrary and the resultant history, judging by the reactions to it, is unacceptable to many professional historians. If a syllabus has to be made lighter, then it has to be restructured and not just axed.

In the textbook for Class XII, there are two parts on themes in Indian history. There is no change in Part I. In Part II, a full chapter of thirty pages is marked as deleted. This is listed as being on 'Kings and Chronicles; the Mughal Courts; Sixteenth and Seventeenth Centuries'. Each page of the booklet is described as a 'list of rationalized content in textbooks for Class XII'. Quite what does this mean?

In trying to understand why half of the history of medieval India—three centuries—is sought to be deleted, it becomes obvious that the deletion fits into the current attempts to obliterate Mughal rule in official history. Mughal rule was previously described as the pinnacle of Muslim rule. Therefore, if the intention is to denigrate Muslim rule, then the Mughal period would be the obvious one to be marginalized if not deleted. But such a decision can only come from those that know little or no history.

Does one have to remind them that whether they like it or not, the period of the sixteenth and seventeenth centuries was one of an immense interface of cultures, economies and social groups? This is demonstrated, for instance, in the flourishing commercial economy manned more often by Jaina and Hindu merchants than those of Arab descent. The nexus between landowners and merchants encouraged the evolution of an impressive economy. Magnificent buildings were a mix of architectural features from sources Indian and other. The imperial court and the courts of their feudatories established excellent ateliers of miniature paintings that vividly reproduced the life of the times and handsomely illustrated the increasing number of books that were being made available in those times. There was no love jihad, so marriages between Hindu Rajput women and Muslim men among the elite were celebrated. The Kacchwaha Rajputs were in any case majorly involved in the top level of administration and politics in the

Mughal empire. Shouldn't Indian citizens today get to know how this and other empires in India were administered, and what were the political patterns encountered by those in high society?

It was a time of immense and impressive new departures in religious ideas, many of which are still identified with in Hindu belief and worship. The Bhakti movement that enormously enriched Hinduism was part of these religious innovations. Sufi sects, other religious sects and groups of Yogis were in dialogue. The dispersal of the ideas that ensued gave form to not only the literature of the time in Hindi and other regional languages but also many aspects of the intellectual life of India in the period prior to the colonial. Hindu and Muslim Krishna-*bhakt*s composed songs that are still sung in the repertoire of classical Indian music. There were wide-ranging studies and exchanges in mathematics, astronomy and medicine that spread to academic centres beyond India and imprinted their cultures as well. Is all this to be wiped out?

Of course, there was the other side of the coin too in the contribution of social laws specific to India. The *Dharma-shastra*s continued to insist on the low status of those outside caste, the *avarna* and the *asprishya* / untouchable, and this carried over into all the religions, resulting in Muslim *pasmanda*s and Sikh *mazhabi*s. Islam may have spoken of the equality of all in the eyes of Allah but the Sharia laws enforced social distances. These were the sections of society that were victimized for over two millennia of our history but by those who belonged to the same religion. References to the condition of the lower castes are deleted in textbooks. Instead, what is stated is the victimization of the Hindus by the Muslims, despite the lack of evidence.

Colonial writers who first wrote modern histories of India deliberately garbled our history and insisted on the validity of the two-nation theory, as set out by James Mill in 1817. This was endorsed as a cornerstone of colonial writing on India. Some Indian historians who were anti-colonial nationalists disagreed with it but did not question it sufficiently. Those that have appropriated this theory and made it basic to their own ideology are the religious nationalists—the creators of Pakistan and the hopefuls that there will be a Hindu Rashtra. This requires the majoritarian rule of Muslims in Pakistan and Hindus in the Hindu Rashtra. Those who write a nuanced history and argue for a critical inquiry and reasoned arguments were and are dismissed by the religious nationalists as the children of Macaulay. Yet the irony of it is that it is precisely the religious nationalists, Muslim and Hindu, who endorse the colonial two-nation theory, inherited directly from colonial authority.

The struggle as reflected in historical writing now goes beyond even the majoritarian ideologies of dominance, whether of Hindu rule or Muslim rule. What we are confronted with is the equally dangerous wiping out of any of the essentials of a methodology in the writing of history or the other social sciences. Methodologies have yet to find their roots in Indian intellectual life. I am surprised by those Indian scientists who claim to base their work on the scientific method but are quite ready to believe the history that has been concocted without any critical enquiry or observance of the historical method. These scientists refer to the history of professional historians, based on evidence, as 'distorted history', or else dismiss it as the wishful thinking of leftists and Marxists, and they happily go on repeating the fantasies of those who are as ignorant of history as they are. They don't pause for a moment to ask whether the historical theories that they support and propound emerge from the use of a scientific method of analysis.

Speaking of which, the NCERT has been hacking away at textbooks in other disciplines too. Darwin's theory of evolution, useful to many disciplines, has been deleted. There isn't even a hint of a suggestion that it should have been discussed prior to deletion. This isn't an issue of left liberals versus the Hindu right, as has been the contention in the history controversy. This concerns a fundamental principle on which many disciplines are based. If the NCERT is going to cut away the foundational principles of reasoned intellectual thought, then there will be nothing left of education, barring knowing the alphabet and numbers 1 to 10. It is already evident that anti-intellectualism is the dominant practice of those in authority. This has been amply demonstrated in the manner in which the history textbooks have been expunged. The question is when will the intellectual and intellectual concerns become assertive again, if only to correct the blatantly incorrect statements made by public persons in public speeches? These latter statements are applauded as correct since the audience knows no better or is too frightened to point out the mistakes. We are living in anti-intellectual times. We seem to have lost our nexus with that which challenges us to think, and think freely.

The question we have to ask ourselves is what do these systematic deletions do to the education of the generation using these books? At one level, as long as education is kept within the boundaries of India, then anything goes. Only Indians will decline educationally. If we produce a generation of non-starters, then it won't make much of a difference to the world. It will make an immense difference to us as Indians. But it is an even more serious matter. Knowledge is advancing rapidly not just in the sciences but also in the humanities. If educated Indians are hoping to keep up, then we cannot get by with reading a history that has gaping holes, is entirely selective in knowing only the history of one Indian community, and is incapable of explaining, in a meaningful way, the world we have lived in and the world we hope to live in. History is the perspective of the evolution of humanity in many ways and the clarity of this perspective relies on the quality of knowledge we use for building our lives.

I am reminded of the experience of contemporary China with what the Chinese government in 1966 called the 'Great Proletarian Cultural Revolution', popularly referred to as the Cultural Revolution. Not only was the discipline of history reconstituted drastically but there was also heavy deletion of old books, scholars and authors, and also that which was said to be Western in origin. There was a strong emphasis on reading and teaching only that which could be said to be indigenous to China. Violent action was taken against those that still harboured old ways of thinking, with mobs deciding on how such persons acting against the Cultural Revolution were to be punished. The 'revolution' failed and was dead within ten years. By 1980, therefore, many Chinese universities had invited scholars from outside to teach in China and re-introduce the knowledge that had been deleted from many disciplines in the country. History had been severely mangled. It was indeed a tremendous intellectual effort for some of us to explain, for instance, an updated version of ancient Indian history to students unaware of even the obvious changes of the previous decade. Deletions do reduce the capacity to think, since evidence is eliminated.

We may go on deleting sections of our history. But in the world outside, there are multiple centres of research into the Indian past, and there are many scholars in those centres. In these centres, the complete Indian history in every detail will continue to be studied with nothing deliberately expunged. They will be subjected to new methods of analyses, will be commented upon, will enrich the understanding of India with new knowledge, and all this will be incorporated into the history of India that will be taught everywhere except in India. We in India will not know anything about that section of Indian history that has been deleted from our books.

Outside India, the multiple cultures of India and their achievements will be studied as part of Indian history and Indian culture, irrespective of the religion of the dynasties that may have presided over the successes or failures. They will be studied in universities, libraries and museums dedicated to the study of India, as a continuation of not only the Indian past but also of the past pertaining to happenings current in various parts of the world. These will have pride of place not only in the history of India but in the history of human achievements. But we in India will be entirely ignorant of their significance since we shall not know them as a part of Indian history nor will they have connections with other histories of the world. These would have been the historical cultures that we today recognize as those with which we had once had exchanges when we created the Indian civilization of past times.

READINGS

ADAMSON, Peter, and Janardan Ganeri. *Classical Indian Philosophy*. New York: Oxford University Press, 2020.

ALAM, Muzaffar. *The Languages of Political Islam: India, 1200–1800*. Chicago: University of Chicago Press, 2004.

——, and Sanjay Subrahmanyam. *Writing the Mughal World: Studies on Culture and Politics*. New York: Columbia University Press, 2012.

ANDERSON, Benedict. *Imagined Communities: Reflections on the Origin and Spread of Nationalism*. London: Verso, 1983.

ANZALDÚA, Gloria. *Borderlands/La Frontera: The New Mestiza*. San Francisco: Aunt Lute Books, 1987.

BANABHATTA. *The Harshacharita of Banabhatta,* 2nd edn (P. V. Kane ed.). New Delhi: Motilal Benarasidass, 1965.

BARTSCH, Shadi. *Plato Goes to China: The Greek Classics and Chinese Nationalism*. Princeton, NJ: Princeton University Press, 2023.

BEACH, Milo Cleveland, Eberhard Fischer, and B. N. Goswamy (eds). *Masters of Indian Painting, 1100–1650*. Delhi: Niyogi Books, 2011.

BEHL, Aditya. *Love's Subtle Magic: An Indian Islamic Literary Tradition, 1379–1545* (Wendy Doniger ed.). New York: Oxford University Press, 2012.

BLOCH, Jules. *Les inscriptions d'Asoka: Traduites et commentées par Jules Bloch*. Paris: Société d'édition, 1950.

BOBBIO, Tommaso. 'Somnatha Mandir in a Play of Mirrors: Heritage, History and the Search for Identity of the New Nation (1842–1951)'. Forthcoming in *The Journal of the Royal Asiatic Society* (2023).

CHAMPAKALAKSHMI, R. *Religion, Tradition and Ideology: Pre-colonial South India*. New Delhi: Oxford University Press, 2011.

CHANDRA, Satish. *Historiography, Religion and State in Medieval India*. New Delhi: Har Anand, 1996.

———. *History of Medieval India, 800–1700*. New Delhi: Orient Blackswan, 2018.

CHATTOPADHYAYA, Debiprasad. *Lokayata: A Study in Ancient Indian Materialism*. New Delhi: People's Publishing House, 1959.

DE ROMANIS, F., and A. Tchernia (eds). *Crossings: Early Mediterranean Contacts with India*. New Delhi: Manohar Publishers / Italian Embassy Cultural Centre, 1997.

DESHPANDE, Madhav P., and Peter Edwin Hook (eds). *Aryan and non-Aryan in India*, Ann Arbor: Center for South and Southeast Asian Studies, University of Michigan, 1978.

EATON, Richard M. *India in the Persianate Age, 1000–1765*. London: Allen Lane, 2019.

ELIOT, Henry Miers, and John Dowson. *History of India, as Told by Its Own Historians*, 8 vols. Delhi: Gyan Publishing, 1996 [1867–77].

ERNST, Carl W. *Refractions of Islam in India: Situating Sufism and Yoga*. New Delhi: Sage / Yoda Press, 2016.

FLOOD, Finbarr B. *Objects of Translation: Material Culture and Medieval 'Hindu–Muslim' Encounter*. Princeton, NJ: Princeton University Press, 2009.

GILMARTIN, David, and Bruce B. Lawrence. *Beyond Turk and Hindu: Rethinking Religious Identities in Islamicate South Asia*. Gainsville: University Press of Florida, 2000.

GOTTSCHALK, Peter. *Beyond Hindu and Muslim: Multiple Identity in Narratives from Village India*. New York: Oxford University Press, 2005.

HILTEBEITEL, Alf. *Dharma*. Honolulu: University of Hawaii Press, 2010.

HOBSBAWM, Eric. *On History*. New York: New Press, 1998.

———. *On Nationalism*. New York: Little, Brown, 2021.

KANGLE, R. P. (ed.). *The Kautilya Arthashastra*. New Delhi: Motilal Benarasidass, 2014.

KING, Richard. *Orientalism and Religion: Post-colonial Theory, India and the 'Mystic East'*. London: Routledge, 1999.

KINRA, Rajeev. *Writing Self, Writing Empire: Chandar Bhan Brahman and the Cultural World of the Indo-Persian State Secretary*. New Delhi: Primus Books, 2016.

LATH, Mukund (trans., annot., introd.). *Ardhakathanaka: Half a Tale*. Jaipur: Rajasthan Prakrit Bharati Sansthan, 1981.

LEE, Joel. 'Who Is the True *Halalkhor*? Genealogy and Ethics in Dalit Muslim Oral Traditions'. *Contributions to Indian Sociology* 52(1) (2018): 1–27.

MAHADEVAN, Iravatham (ed. and trans.). *Early Tamil Epigraphy: From the Earliest Times to the Sixth Century AD*. Cambridge, MA: Harvard University Press, 2003.

MAX MÜLLER, Friedrich. *India: What Can It Teach Us?* New York, 1883. Available at: https://bit.ly/43MduEa (last accessed 18 June 2023).

MERUTUNGA. *Prabandhacintamani, or Wishing-Stone of Narratives* (C. H. Tawney trans.). Calcutta: Asiatic Society, 1901.

MILL, James. *The History of British India*, 3 vols. London, 1817–23. Available at: https://bit.ly/3NAguhf (last accessed 18 June 2023).

MIR, Farina. 'Genre and Devotion in Punjabi Popular Narratives: Rethinking Cultural and Religious Syncretism'. *Comparative Studies in Society and History* 48(3) (2006): 727–58.

OBER, Josiah. *Political Dissent in Democratic Athens: Intellectual Critics of Popular Rule.* Princeton, NJ: Princeton University Press, 1998.

OLIVELLE, Patrick (trans.) *Dharmasutras: The Law Codes of Ancient India.* New York: Oxford University Press, 1999.

PRASAD, Pushpa. *Sanskrit Inscriptions of the Delhi Sultanate, 1191–1526.* New Delhi: Oxford University Press, 1990.

ROY, Kumkum. *The Emergence of Monarchy in North India, Eighth to Fourth Centuries BC: As Reflected in the Brahmanical Tradition.* New Delhi: Oxford University Press, 1994.

SAID, Edward. *Orientalism.* New York: Pantheon Books, 1978.

SANDERSON, Alexis. 'Tolerance, Exclusivity, Inclusivity and Persecution in Indian Religion during the Early Medieval Period', in John Makinson (ed.), *Honoris Causa: Essays in Honour of Aveek Sarkar.* London: Allen Lane, 2015, pp. 155–224.

SHAH, A. M. 'Sects and Hindu Social Structure' in *Contributions to Indian Society* 40(2) (2006): 209–48.

SHARMA, Sri Ram. *The Religious Policy of the Mughal Emperors.* New York: Asia Publishing House, 1972 [1940]. Available at: https://bit.ly/3NcFauR (last accessed 18 June 2023).

SIRCAR, D. C. (ed.). *Select Inscriptions Bearing on Indian History and Civilization, Volume 2.* New Delhi: Motilal Benarasidass, 1983.

——, and B. C. Chhabra (eds). 'Rashtrakuta Charters from Chinchani'. *Epigraphia Indica* 32 (1957–58): 45–55. Available at: https://bit.ly/3JkKzir (last accessed 18 June 2023).

SKJÆRVØ, Prods Oktor. *The Spirit of Zoroastrianism.* New Haven, CT: Yale University Press, 2011.

SONTHEIMER, Günther-Dietz, and Hermann Kulke (eds). *Hinduism Reconsidered.* New Delhi: Manohar, 2001.

STEIN, M. A. (ed.). *Kalhana's Rajatarangini: A Chronicle of the Kings of Kashmir.* New Delhi: Motilal Benarasidass, 1979 [1892].

TALBOT, Cynthia. *Precolonial India in Practice: Society, Region, and Identity in Medieval Andhra.* New Delhi: Oxford University Press, 2001.

TANEJA, Anand Vivek. *Jinneology: Time, Islam, and Ecological Thought in the Medieval Ruins of Delhi.* Stanford, CA: Stanford University Press, 2018.

THAPAR, Romila. *Asoka and the Decline of the Mauryas,* 2ND EDN. New Delhi: Oxford University Press, 2012.

——. *From Lineage to State: Social Formations of the Mid-First Millennium BC in the Ganga Valley.* New Delhi: Oxford University Press, 1991.

————. *Interpreting Early India*. New Delhi: Oxford University Press, 1993.

————. *Somanatha: The Many Voices of a History*. New Delhi: Penguin Books, 2008.

————, Michael Witzel, Jaya Menon, Kai Friese, and Razib Khan. *Which of Us Are Aryans? Five Experts Challenge the Controversial Aryan* Question. New Delhi: Aleph, 2019.

TRUSCHKE, Audrey. 'Contested History: Brahmanical Memories of Relations with the Mughals'. *Journal of the Economic and Social History of the Orient* 58(4) (2015): 419–52.

————. 'Hindu: A History'. *Comparative Studies in Society and History* 65(2) (2023): 1–26.

VERARDI, Giovanni. *Hardships and Downfall of Buddhism in India*. New Delhi: Manohar, 2011.

WATTERS, Thomas. *On Yuan Chwang's Travels in India, 629–645 AD*. London: Royal Asiatic Society, 1904. Available at: https://bit.ly/46803QH (last accessed 18 June 2023).

YAZDANI, Ghulam. *The Early History of the Deccan*, 2 vols. New Delhi: Munshiram Manoharlal, 1982.